NINJA FOODI GRILL COOKBOOK FOR BEGINNERS

250 Mouthwatering And Easy-To-Make, Recipes to Cook Your Food In 1250 Different Ways. Learn The Smart Way To Air Fry, Bake, And Grill Indoor Effortlessly

Sophia Smith

Table of Contents

Introduction

What is the Tender Crisp Technology?

Cooking tougher ingredients or meats with pressure cooking makes them into much tender and delicious food. On the other hand, air frying makes our food crispier and have a tasty crust in it. The combo of both air frying and pressure cooking is the basic working principle of Ninja Foodi and is called the Tender Crisp Technology. It creates a perfect tender and juicy food that is crispy on its outer surface. The cooking procedures initiate with pressure cooking, followed by a customized air frying standard to achieve the crispiness of your choice.

Tender Crisp Technology utilizes steam (super-heated) to infuse both flavor and moisture faster into the food cooked with pressure cooking. Afterward, the crisping lid blows down hot air to every corner of your food, and makes it crispier and finishes it with a certain golden color that can't be achieved by any other cooking appliance.

How to use the Ninja Foodi?

The food with the Ninja Foodi is the best both a pressure cooker and air fryer can give you, but this time it's going to be in a single pot. You can prepare wholesome food with multi-texture 360 meals by preparing vegetables, grains, and proteins in a single go.

Modern electric pressure cookers can help you simplify everyday food preparation; therefore, learning to use Ninja Foodi can be both beneficial and fun! It may sound like a fancy electric pressure cooker, but your Ninja Foodi takes it even further with its awesome capabilities. While Ninja Foodi has the basic pressure cooker function, it can also air and steam fry your food and bake it using unique heating elements.

Generally, the Ninja Foodi consists of a 6.5-quart removable cooking pot, Cook & Crisp Basket, a pressure lid, and a crisping lid. When it comes to its most important parts and accessories, it is equipped with handles, pressure release valve, red float valve, silicone ring, reversible rack, detachable diffuser, heat shield, cooker base, anti-clog cap, air outlet vent, condensation collector, power cord, and sensor. Accessories that are sold separately include Cook & Crisp™ layered insert, loaf pan, crisper pan, multi-purpose pan, roasting rack insert, and dehydrating rack.

Your Ninja Foodi also has built-in multiple safety features. However, always use caution when opening the lid; never place your face and hands over the unit and use heat-resistant oven mitts.

You will have an electric pressure cooker and air fryer in one! It has two lids, which allow you to pressure cook and crisp in the same cooking pot. Use a pressure lid with functions such as pressure cook, slow cook, and steam. Use a crisping lid with functions such as air crisp, broil, bake, and roast. Use the "SEAR/SAUTE" function with an open lid.

That being said, this particular book has been designed to help beginners get a grip on the appliance, and keeping that in mind, the first chapter of the book covers all the basic information that you might need to know regarding the Ninja Foodi Grill.

So, what are you waiting for? Jump right in and start exploring!

What Is Ninja Foodi Grill?

The Ninja Foodi is the most versatile and easy to use kitchen appliance you will ever own. It's an electric pressure cooker, sauté pan, air fryer, slow cooker, a rice cooker all in one. The combination of air fryer and pressure cooker will cook your food faster and more efficiently than any other tool in your kitchen. You can make all your favorite meals in the Ninja Foodi Cooker.

The Ninja Foodi Cooker is top-notch. You will be fascinated by how well it cooks your favorite food. It works fast; it is easy to set up and use in the kitchen. Therefore, if you're new to using a multi-cooker, you'll get used to it quickly and easily. You can use your multi-cooker manually or opt for some of the seven preset programs. Programs. An easy-to-use interface allows you to select your desired cooking program easily.

Ninja Foodi Functionalities

The list below offers a brief look at all the core buttons´ functionalities that should help you understand what each of the main buttons does.

Pressure

Let's first talk about the single feature that you will be using most of the time. The Pressure function will allow you to use your Ninja Foodi as a Pressure Cooker appliance and cook your meals as you would in an electric pressure cooker such as the Ninja Foodi.

In this feature, foods are cooked at high temperatures under pressure.

Just make sure to be careful when releasing the pressure! Otherwise, you might harm yourself.

Steam

Asides from Air Crisp, the Steam Function is probably one of the healthiest cooking options available in the Foodi!

The basic principle is as follows: water is boiled inside the Ninja Foodi that generates a good steam amount. This hot steam is then used for cooking your ingredients kept in a steaming rack situated at the top of your pot´s inner chamber.

Steaming is perfect for vegetables and other tender foods as it allows you to preserve the nutrients while maintaining a nice crispy correctly.

Asides from vegetables, however, the Steam function can also be used for cooking various fish and seafood, which are much more delicate than other red meats and chicken.

The steaming fish process is the same; all you have to do is place them on the steaming rack.

Steaming the fish helps to preserve the flavor and moisture as well perfectly.

Slow Cooker

Despite popular belief, some foods tend to taste a whole lot better when slowly cooked over a shallow temperature for hours on end. This is why Slow Cookers, such as the Crockpot, are so popular amongst chefs and house makers!

The Slow Cooker feature of the Ninja Foodi allows you to achieve the same result with a different appliance.

Ideal scenarios to use the Slow Cooker function would be when you want to cook your foods for longer to bring out the intense flavor of spices and herbs in stews, soups, and casseroles.

Since it takes a lot of time to Slow Cook, you should prepare and toss the ingredients early on before your feeding time.

For example, if you want to have your Slow Cooker meal for breakfast, prepare ingredients the night before and add them to your Foodi. The Foodi will do its magic and have the meal prepared by morning.

The Slow Cooker feature also comes with a HIGH or LOW setting that allows you to decide how long you want your meal to simmer.

Air Crisp

This is probably the feature that makes the Ninja Foodi so revolutionary and awesome to use! The Tender crisp lid that comes as a part of the Ninja Foodi allows you to use the appliance as the perfect Air Fryer device.

Using the Tender crisp lid and Air Crisp mode, the appliance will let you bake, roast, broil meals to perfection using just the power of superheated air! In the end, you will get perfectly caramelized, heartwarming dishes.

The Foodi comes with a dedicated crisping basket specifically designed for this purpose, which optimizes the way meals are air fried in the Foodi.

But the best part of all of these is probably the fact that it is using the Air Crisp feature; you will be able to cook your meals using almost none to minimal amount of oil!

It is also possible to combine both the pressure-cooking mechanism and the Air Crisp function to create unique and flavorful dishes.

The Pressure-cooking phase will help you to seal the delicious juices of the meal inside the meat. Simultaneously, the crisping lid and Air Crisp mechanism will allow you to cook/roast your meal to perfection, giving a nice heartfelt crispy finish.

This combined method is also amazing when roasting whole chicken meat or roasts, as all the moisture remains intact, and the final result turns out to be a dramatic crispy finish.

Sear/Sauté

The Browning/Sauté or Sear/Sauté mode of the Ninja Foodi provides you with the means to brown your meat before cooking it using just a little oil. This is similar to when you are browning meat on a stovetop frying pan. And keeping that in mind, the Ninja Foodie's browning model comes with five different Stove Top temperature settings that allow you to set your desired settings with ease.

Asides from browning meat, the different Stove Top temperatures also allow you to gently simmer your foods, cook or even sear them at very high temperatures.

Searing is yet another way to infuse your meat´s delicious flavors inside and give an extremely satisfying result.

This particular model is also excellent if you are in the mode for a quick Sautéed vegetable snack to go along with your main course.

Bake/Roast

To those who love to bake, this function is a dream come true! The Bake/Roast function allows the Foodi to be used as a traditional convection oven. This means you will be do anything that you might do with a general everyday oven! If you are in the mode to bake amazing cakes or casseroles, the Foodi has got you covered!

Broil

The broil function´s primary purpose is to allow you to use your appliance like an oven broiler and slightly brown the top of your dish if required. If you are in the mood for roasting a fine piece of pork loin to perfection or broiling your dish until the cheese melts and oozes, this mode is the perfect one to go with!

Dehydrate

In some more premium models of the Ninja Foodi appliance, you will notice a function labeled as "Dehydrate." This particular function is best suited for simple dried snacks such as dried apple slices, banana chips, jerky, etc. As you can probably guess, this function´s core idea is to suck out the moisture and dehydrate your ingredient into a hearty edible snack.

Start/Stop Button

This particular button´s function is pretty straightforward; it allows you to initiate or stop the cooking process.

How to Use the Ninja Foodi Grill

When you cook for the first time with your Foodi grill, you must first wash the detachable cooking parts with warm soapy water to remove any oil and debris. Let them air dry and place them back inside once you are ready to cook. An easy-to-follow instruction guide comes with each unit, so make sure to go over it before cooking.

Position your grill on a level and secure surface. Leave at least 6 inches of space around it, especially at the back where the air intake vent and air socket are located. Ensure that the splatter guard is installed whenever the grill is in use. This is a wire mesh that covers the heating element on the inside of the lid.

For grilling:

- Plug your unit into an outlet and power on the grill.
- Use the grill grate over the cooking pot and choose the grill function. This has four default temperature settings of low at 400 degrees F, medium at 450 degrees F, high at 500 degrees F, and max at 510 degrees F.
- Set the time needed to cook. You may check the grilling cheat sheet that comes with your unit to guide you with the time and temperature settings. It is best to check the food regularly depending on the doneness you prefer and to avoid overcooking.
- Once the required settings are selected, press start and wait for the digital display to show 'add food'. The unit will start to preheat similar to an oven and will show the progress through the display. This step takes about 8 minutes.

- If you need to check the food or flip it, the timer will pause and resume once the lid is closed.
- The screen will show 'Done' once the timer and cooking have been completed. Power off the unit and unplug the device. Leave the hood open to let the unit cool faster.

For roasting:

- Remove the grill grates and use the cooking pot that comes with the unit. You may also purchase their roasting rack for this purpose.
- Press the roast option and set the timer between 1 to 4 hours depending on the recipe requirements. The Foodi will preheat for 3 minutes regardless of the time you have set.
- Once ready, place the meat directly on the roasting pot or rack.
- Check occasionally for doneness. A meat thermometer is another useful tool to get your meats perfectly cooked.

For baking:

- Remove the grates and use the cooking pot.
- Choose the bake setting and set your preferred temperature and time. Preheating will take about 3 minutes.
- Once done with preheating, you may put the ingredients directly on the cooking pot, or you may use your regular baking tray. An 8-inch baking tray can fit inside as well as similar-sized oven-safe containers.

For air frying/air crisping:

- Put the crisper basket in and close the lid.

- Press the air crisp or air fry option then the start button. The default temperature is set at 390° F and will preheat at about 3 minutes. You can adjust the temperature and time by pressing the buttons beside these options.
- If you do not need to preheat, just press the air crisp button a second time and the display will show you the 'add food' message.
- Put the food inside and shake or turn every 10 minutes. Use oven mitts or tongs with silicone tips when doing this.

For dehydrating:

- Place the first layer of food directly on the cooking pot.

- Add the crisper basket and add one more layer.
- Choose the dehydrate setting and set the timer between 7 to 10 hours.
- You may check the progress from time to time.

For cooking frozen foods:

- Choose the medium heat, which is 450° F using the grill option. You may also use the air crisp option if you are cooking fries, vegetables, and other frozen foods.
- Set the time needed for your recipe. Add a few minutes to compensate for the thawing.
- Flip or shake after a few minutes to cook the food evenly.

Cleaning and Maintenance

Components are dishwasher-safe and are fabricated with a non-stick ceramic coating, to make clean-up and maintenance easier. Plus,

the grill conveniently comes with a plastic cleaning brush with a scraper at the other end.

Cleaning tips:

1. Let the grill cool down completely and ensure that it is unplugged from the power outlet before trying to clean the unit.
2. Take out the splatter guard, grill grates, and cooking pot, and soak in soapy water for a few hours to let the debris soften and make cleaning easier. Wash only the removable parts.
3. Gently brush off dirt and debris using the plastic brush that comes with your grill. Use the other end of the brush to dislodge food in hard to reach areas.
4. Let the parts dry thoroughly.
5. Clean the insides and exterior of the unit with a clean damp cloth.

Maintenance tips:

1. Always keep your unit clean, especially before putting in a new batch for cooking. You should clean the parts and the unit after each use.

2. Never use cleaning instruments or chemicals that are too harsh and can damage the coating.
3. Keep the electrical cords away from children and any traffic in your kitchen.
4. Avoid getting the unit and electrical components wet and place them away from areas that constantly get soaked or damp.
5. Always unplug the unit when not in use.

Troubleshooting:

1. Smoke coming out of the grill
2. Although the Ninja Foodi is virtually smokeless as advertised, you may see some smoke from time to time for several reasons.
3. One is the type of oil you use for cooking. Ideally, canola, grape seed, and avocado oil should be used since they have a high smoke point. This means that they do not produce smoke or burn at high temperatures. Other oils with high smoke points include corn, almond, safflower, sesame, and sunflower oils.
4. Another reason is the accumulation of grease at the bottom of the pot. If you continuously cook foods that produce a lot of grease and oil, this will burn and create smoke. Empty and clean the pot before cooking the next batch.
5. The grill is showing 'Add Food'
6. This means that the unit has finished preheating and that you can now put food inside the grill.
7. The control panel is showing 'Shut Lid'
8. Try opening the lid and closing it securely until the message is gone.
9. Unit is unresponsive and only showing 'E' on the panel
10. Your unit is damaged and you need to contact customer service.

Tips and Frequently Asked Questions

Here are some useful tips you can use when cooking with the Ninja Foodi and some commonly asked questions to guide you if you are planning to purchase one for yourself.

Useful tips:

- Brush or spray the grates with some canola, corn, or avocado oil to avoid smoke.
- A light coating of oil will make your air-fried French fries taste better.
- Use the time charts as a guide but make sure you check the food regularly since the grill gets hot and can cook quickly. You may also use a meat thermometer for your food to cook exactly the way you want.
- Use silicone or wooden utensils. Never stick metal tongs or cutleries on your grill to avoid electric shock and damaging the ceramic coating.
- If you are planning to do a lot of dehydrating and baking, it will be helpful to purchase their food rack and baking pan.
- If the timer was up but you need to cook the food longer, simply adjust the timer and press the start button to continue cooking.
- Although preheating is recommended to get the finest results, you can skip this step by pressing the option a second time.
- To get juicier meat, let it rest at least 5 minutes before slicing.

FAQs

1. Is it worth the price?

If you are getting the Foodi grill as a secondary appliance, it may seem pricey. But given the various functions, you are getting with one piece of equipment, the value for money will be apparent with continuous use.

2. Can it heat the kitchen as most ovens do?

No. One great thing about portable cookers like the Ninja Foodi grill is that it does not make the kitchen uncomfortably hot making it ideal for use even during summer.

3. What button should I press to pause the timer?

Opening the lid will automatically pause the timer.

4. Why is my food not evenly cooked when air-fried?

It is best not to overcrowd food inside the crisper basket and create an even layer to get better results. You need to flip or shake the food every few minutes to have even browning.

5. How do I convert cooking temperatures from recipes meant for regular ovens?

You can simply reduce the temperature required by 25 degrees Fahrenheit when using the Ninja Foodi grill. You will have to check the food regularly to make sure it will not get overcooked.

Oil	Smoke Point ºF	Smoke Point °C
Refined Avocado Oil	520ºF	270°C
Safflower Oil	510ºF	265ºC
Rice Bran Oil	490ºF	254ºC
Refined or Light Olive Oil	465ºF	240ºC
Soybean Oil	450ºF	232ºC
Peanut Oil	450ºF	232ºC
Ghee or Clarified Butter	450ºF	232ºC
Corn Oil	450ºF	232ºC
Refined Coconut Oil	450ºF	232ºC
Safflower Oil	440ºF	227ºC
Refined Sesame Oil	410ºF	210ºC
Vegetable Oil	400-450ºF	204-232ºC
Beef Tallow	400ºF	204ºC
Canola Oil	400ºF	204ºC
Grapeseed Oil	390ºF	199ºC
Unrefined or Virgin Avocado Oil	375ºF	190ºC
Pork Fat or Lard	370ºF	188ºC
Chicken Fat or Schmaltz	375ºF	190ºC
Duck Fat	375ºF	190ºC
Vegetable Shortening	360ºF	182ºC
Unrefined Sesame Oil	350ºF	177ºC
Extra Virgin or Unrefined Coconut Oil	350ºF	177ºC
Extra Virgin Olive Oil	325-375ºF	163-190ºC
Butter	302ºF	150ºC

Breakfast

Homemade Yogurt

Preparation Time: 15 minutes

Cooking Time: 12 Hours

Servings: 8

Ingredients:

- ½ gallon whole milk
- 2 tablespoons plain yogurt with active live cultures
- 1 tablespoon vanilla extract (optional)
- ½ cup honey (optional)

Directions:

1. Pour the milk into the pot. Assemble the Pressure Lid, making sure the pressure release valve is in the Vent position. Select Sear/Sauté and set it to Medium. Select Start/Stop to begin.
2. Bring the milk to 180°F, checking the temperature often and stirring frequently so the milk does not burn at the bottom. Select Start/Stop to turn off Sear/Sauté.
3. Allow the milk to cool to 110°F, continuing to check the temperature often and stirring frequently. Gently skim off the "skin" on the milk and discard.
4. Stir in the yogurt and whisk until incorporated.
5. Assemble the Pressure Lid, making sure the pressure release valve is in the Vent position. Let incubate for 8 hours.
6. After 8 hours, transfer the yogurt to a glass container and chill for 4 hours in the refrigerator.

7. Add the vanilla and honey (if using) to the yogurt and mix until well combined. Cover and place the glass bowl back in the refrigerator or divide the yogurt among airtight glass jars.

TIP: If you prefer a thicker Greek-style yogurt, let the yogurt strain through cheesecloth into a large mixing bowl overnight in the refrigerator.

Nutrition: Calories: 149; Total fat: 8g; Saturated fat: 5g; Cholesterol: 25mg; Sodium: 99mg; Carbohydrates: 13g; Fiber: 0g; Protein: 8g

Hard-Boiled Eggs

Preparation Time: 2 minutes

Cooking Time: 15 Minutes

Servings: 2-12 eggs

Ingredients:

- 1 cup of water
- 2 to 12 eggs

Directions:

1. Place the Reversible Rack in the pot in the lower position. Add the water and arrange the eggs on the rack in a single layer.
2. Assemble the Pressure Lid, making sure the pressure release valve is in the Seal position. Select Pressure and set to Low. Set the time to 8 minutes. Select Start/Stop to begin.
3. While the eggs are cooking, prepare a large bowl of ice water.
4. When pressure cooking is complete, quick release the pressure by moving the pressure release valve to the Vent position. Carefully remove the lid when the unit has finished releasing pressure.
5. Using a slotted spoon, immediately transfer the eggs to the ice water bath and allow to cool for 5 minutes.

TIP: Hard-boiled eggs with hard yolks are ideal for deviled eggs, but if you prefer runny yolks, then you will want soft-boiled eggs. For soft-boiled eggs, cook on Low for 2 to 3 minutes, and for medium-boiled eggs, cook on Low for 5 to 6 minutes.

Nutrition: (1 egg) Calories: 71; Total fat: 5g; Saturated fat: 2g; Cholesterol: 211mg; Sodium: 70mg; Carbohydrates: 0g; Fiber: 0g; Protein: 6g

Easy Cheesy Egg Bake

Preparation Time: 5 minutes

Cooking Time: 27 Minutes

Servings: 4

Ingredients:

- 4 eggs
- 1 cup milk
- 1 teaspoon sea salt
- 1 teaspoon freshly ground black pepper
- 1 cup shredded Cheddar cheese
- 1 red bell pepper, seeded and chopped
- 8 ounces ham, chopped
- 1 cup of water

Directions:

1. In a medium mixing bowl, whisk together the eggs, milk, salt, and black pepper. Stir in the Cheddar cheese.
2. Place the bell pepper and ham in the Multi-Purpose Pan or an 8-inch baking pan. Pour the egg mixture over the pepper and ham. Cover the pan with aluminum foil and place it on the Reversible Rack.
3. Pour the water into the pot. Place the rack with the pan in the pot in the lower position.
4. Assemble the Pressure Lid, making sure the pressure release valve is in the Seal position. Select Pressure and set to High. Set the time to 20 minutes. Select Start/Stop to begin.

5. When pressure cooking is complete, quick release the pressure by moving the pressure release valve to the Vent position. Carefully remove the lid when the unit has finished releasing pressure.
6. When cooking is complete, remove the pan from the pot and place it on a cooling rack. Let cool for 5 minutes, then serve.

TIP: Swap the red bell pepper for other veggies like broccoli, spinach, and onions, but stay away from those that will release water, like tomatoes, zucchini, and mushrooms. Chicken and smoked sausage make good substitutes for the ham.

Nutrition: Calories: 332; Total fat: 21g; Saturated fat: 10g; Cholesterol: 280mg; Sodium: 1693mg; Carbohydrates: 6g; Fiber: 1g; Protein: 28g

Crispy Bacon Hash and Baked Eggs

Preparation Time: 10 minutes

Cooking Time: 40 Minutes

Servings: 4

Ingredients:

- 6 slices bacon, chopped
- 1 yellow onion, diced
- 2 russet potatoes, peeled and diced
- 1 teaspoon paprika
- 1 teaspoon sea salt
- 1 teaspoon freshly ground black pepper
- 1 teaspoon garlic salt
- 4 eggs

Directions:

1. Select Sear/Sauté and set it to Medium-High. Select Start/Stop to begin. Allow the pot to preheat for 5 minutes.

2. Once hot, add the bacon to the pot. Cook, stirring occasionally, for 5 minutes, or until the bacon is crispy.
3. Add the onion and potatoes to the pot. Sprinkle with paprika, sea salt, pepper, and garlic salt.
4. Close the Crisping Lid. Select Bake/Roast, set the temperature to 350°F, and set the time to 25 minutes. Cook, stirring occasionally until the potatoes are tender and golden brown.
5. Crack the eggs onto the surface of the hash. Close the Crisping Lid. Select Bake/Roast, set the temperature to 350°F, and set the time to 10 minutes.
6. Check the eggs after 3 minutes. Continue cooking for the remaining 7 minutes, checking occasionally, until your desired doneness is achieved. Serve immediately.

Nutrition: Calories: 364; Total fat: 24g; Saturated fat: 8g; Cholesterol: 240mg; Sodium: 1008mg; Carbohydrates: 24g; Fiber: 2g; Protein: 14g

Upside-Down Broccoli and Cheese Quiche

Preparation Time: 10 minutes

Cooking Time: 20 Minutes

Servings: 6

Ingredients:

- 8 eggs
- ½ cup milk
- 1 teaspoon sea salt
- 1 teaspoon freshly ground black pepper
- 1 cup shredded Cheddar cheese
- 1 tablespoon extra-virgin olive oil
- 1 yellow onion, chopped
- 2 garlic cloves, minced
- 2 cups thinly sliced broccoli florets
- 1 refrigerated piecrust, at room temperature

Directions:

1. Select Sear/Sauté and set to High. Select Start/Stop it to begin. Allow the pot to preheat for 5 minutes.
2. In a large mixing bowl, whisk together the eggs, milk, salt, and pepper. Stir in the Cheddar cheese.
3. Put the oil, onion, and garlic in the preheated pot and stir occasionally for 5 minutes. Add the broccoli florets and sauté for another 5 minutes.
4. Pour the egg mixture over the vegetables and gently stir for 1 minute (this will allow the egg mixture to temper well and ensure that it cooks evenly under the crust).
5. Lay the piecrust evenly on top of the filling mixture, folding over the edges if necessary. Make a small cut in the center of the piecrust so that steam can escape during baking.
6. Close the Crisping Lid. Select Broil and set the time to 10 minutes. Select Start/Stop to begin.
7. When cooking is complete, remove the pot and place it on a heat-resistant surface. Let the quiche rest for 5 to 10 minutes before serving.

Nutrition: Calories: 393; Total fat: 26g; Saturated fat: 10g; Cholesterol: 304mg; Sodium: 773mg; Carbohydrates: 26g; Fiber: 2g; Protein: 16g

Simple Strawberry Jam

Preparation Time: 10 minutes

Cooking Time: 42 Minutes

Servings: 1 ½ Cups

Ingredients:

- 2 pounds strawberries, hulled and halved
- Juice of 2 lemons
- 1½ cups granulated sugar

Directions:

1. Place the strawberries, lemon juice, and sugar in the pot. Using a silicone potato masher, mash the ingredients together to begin to release the strawberry juices.
2. Assemble the Pressure Lid, making sure the pressure release valve is in the Seal position. Select Pressure and set to High. Set the time to 1 minute. Select Start/Stop to begin.
3. When pressure cooking is complete, allow the pressure to naturally release for 10 minutes, then quickly release any remaining pressure by moving the pressure release valve to the Vent position. Carefully remove the lid when the pressure has finished releasing.
4. Select Sear/Sauté and set it to Medium-High. Select Start/Stop to begin. Allow the jam to reduce for 20 minutes, or until it tightens.
5. Mash the strawberries using the silicone potato masher for a textured jam, or transfer the strawberry mixture to a food processor and purée for a smooth consistency. Let the jam cool, pour it into a glass jar, and refrigerate for up to 2 weeks.

TIP: This natural jam may be a bit looser than store-bought versions because it uses all whole ingredients. If you prefer to thicken the jam, stir in flavorless gelatin after step 4.

Nutrition: (1 tablespoon) Calories: 23; Total fat: 0g; Saturated fat: 0g; Cholesterol: 0mg; Sodium: 0mg; Carbohydrates: 6g; Fiber: 0g; Protein: 0g

Apple-Cranberry Oatmeal

Preparation Time: 5 minutes

Cooking Time: 27 Minutes

Servings: 4

Ingredients:

- 2 cups gluten-free steel-cut oats
- 3¾ cups water

- ¼ cup apple cider vinegar
- 1 tablespoon ground cinnamon
- ½ teaspoon ground nutmeg
- ½ teaspoon vanilla extract
- ½ cup dried cranberries, plus more for garnish
- 2 apples, peeled, cored, and diced
- 1/8 teaspoon sea salt
- Maple syrup, for topping

Directions:

1. Add the oats, water, vinegar, cinnamon, nutmeg, vanilla, cranberries, apples, and salt to the pot. Assemble the Pressure Lid, making sure the pressure release valve is in the Seal position. Select Pressure and set to High. Set the time to 11 minutes. Select Start/Stop to begin.
2. When pressure cooking is complete, allow the pressure to naturally release for 10 minutes, then quickly release any remaining pressure by moving the pressure release valve to the Vent position. Carefully remove the lid when the pressure has finished releasing.
3. Stir the oatmeal and serve immediately. Top with maple syrup and more dried cranberries, as desired.

TIP: If you prefer old-fashioned oats, you can substitute an equal amount of them for the steel-cut oats and reduce pressure Cooking Time to 6 minutes. You can also add more water if you prefer thinner oatmeal.

Nutrition: Calories: 399; Total fat: 6g; Saturated fat: 1g; Cholesterol: 0mg; Sodium: 76mg; Carbohydrates: 71g; Fiber: 12g; Protein: 14g

Breakfast Frittata

Preparation time: 35 minutes

Cooking Time: 40 minutes

Servings: 2

Ingredients:

- 1/4 lb. breakfast sausage, cooked and crumbled
- 4 eggs, beaten
- 1/2 cup cheddar cheese, shredded
- 1 red bell pepper, diced
- 1 green onion, chopped
- Cooking spray

Directions:

1. Mix the eggs, sausage, cheese, onion, and bell pepper.
2. Spray a small baking pan with oil. Pour the egg mixture into the pan.
3. Set the basket inside. Close the crisping lid.
4. Choose air crisp function. Cook at 360 degrees F for 20 minutes.

Nutrition: Calories 380, Total Fat 27.4g, Saturated Fat 12.0g, Cholesterol 443mg, Sodium 694mg, Total Carbohydrates 2.9g, Dietary Fiber 0.4g, Protein 31.2g, Sugars 1g, Potassium 328mg

Egg in Toast

Preparation time: 15 minutes

Cooking Time: 20 minutes

Servings: 1

Ingredients:

- 1 slice of bread
- 1 egg
- Salt and pepper to taste
- Cooking spray

Directions:

1. Spray a small baking pan with oil. Place the bread inside the pan.
2. Make a hole in the middle of the bread slice.
3. Cracks open the egg and put it inside the hole.
4. Cover with the crisping lid. Set it to air crisp.

5. Cook at 330 degrees for 6 minutes. Flip the toast and cook for 3 more minutes.

Nutrition: Calories 92, Total Fat 5.2g, Saturated Fat 1.5g, Cholesterol 164mg, Sodium 123mg, Total Carbohydrate 5g, Dietary Fiber 0.3g, Total Sugars 0.7g, Protein 6.2g, Potassium 69mg

Baked Eggs

Preparation time: 10 minutes

Cooking Time: 15 minutes

Servings: 1

Ingredients:

- Cooking spray
- 1 egg
- 1 tsp. dried rosemary
- Salt and pepper to taste

Directions:

1. Coat a ramekin with oil. Crack the egg into the ramekin.
2. Season with rosemary, salt, and pepper.
3. Close the crisping lid. Set it to air crisp. Cook at 330 degrees F for 5 minutes.

Nutrition: Calories 72, Total Fat 5.1g, Saturated Fat 1.5g, Cholesterol 164mg, Sodium 62mg, Total Carbohydrate 1.2g, Dietary Fiber 0.5g, Total Sugars 0.3g, Protein 5.6g, Potassium 72mg

Breakfast Potatoes

Preparation time: 1 hour and 10 minutes

Cooking Time: 1 hour and 20 minutes

Servings: 2

Ingredients:

- 2 potatoes, scrubbed, rinsed, and diced
- 1 tablespoon olive oil
- Salt to taste
- 1/4 teaspoon garlic powder

Directions:

1. Put the potatoes in a bowl of cold water. Soak for 45 minutes.
2. Pat the potatoes dry with a paper towel. Toss in olive oil, salt, and garlic powder.
3. Put in the basket. Seal the crisping lid. Set it to air crisp.
4. Cook at 400 degrees for 20 minutes. Flip the potatoes halfway through.

Nutrition: Calories 208, Total Fat 7.2g, Saturated Fat 1.1g, Cholesterol 0mg, Sodium 90mg, Total Carbohydrate 33.7g, Dietary Fiber 5.1g, Total Sugars 2.5g, Protein 3.6g, Potassium 871mg

Egg & Turkey Sausage Cups

Preparation time: 20 minutes

Cooking Time: 25 minutes

Servings: 4

Ingredients:

- 8 tablespoons turkey sausage, cooked and crumbled, divided
- 8 tablespoons frozen spinach, chopped and divided
- 8 teaspoons shredded cheddar cheese, divided
- 4 eggs

Directions:

1. Add a layer of the sausage, spinach, and cheese to each muffin cup.
2. Crack the egg open on top. Seal the crisping lid. Set it to air crisp.
3. Cook at 330 degrees for 10 minutes.

Nutrition: Calories 171, Total Fat 13.3g, Saturated Fat 4.7g, Cholesterol 190mg, Sodium 289mg, Total Carbohydrate 0.5g, Dietary Fiber 0.1g, Total Sugars 0.4g, Protein 11.9g, Potassium 161mg

Omelets

Preparation time: 15 minutes

Cooking Time: 20 minutes

Servings: 2

Ingredients:

- 2 eggs
- 1/4 cup milk
- 1 tablespoon red bell pepper, chopped
- 1 slice ham, diced
- 1 tablespoon mushrooms, chopped
- Salt to taste
- 1/4 cup cheese, shredded

Directions:

1. Whisk the eggs and milk in a bowl. Add the ham and vegetables. Season with salt.
2. Pour the mixture into a small pan. Place the pan inside the basket.
3. Seal the crisping lid. Set it to air crisp. Cook at 350 degrees for 8 minutes.
4. Before it is fully cooked, sprinkle the cheese on top.
5. Coat the beef cubes with salt and pickling spice.
6. In a skillet over medium heat, pour in the olive oil.

Nutrition: Calories 177, Total Fat 11g, Saturated Fat 5.1g, Cholesterol 189mg, Sodium 425mg, Total Carbohydrate 7.1g, Dietary Fiber 1g, Total Sugars 4.8g, Protein 13.1g, Potassium 249mg

Cheesy Broccoli Quiche

Preparation time: 40 minutes

Cooking Time: 45 minutes

Servings: 2

Ingredients:

- 1 cup of water
- 2 cups broccoli florets
- 1 carrot, chopped
- 1 cup cheddar cheese, grated
- 1/4 cup Feta cheese, crumbled
- 1/4 cup milk
- 2 eggs
- 1 teaspoon parsley
- 1 teaspoon thyme
- Salt and pepper to taste

Directions:

1. Pour the water inside. Place the basket inside.
2. Put the carrots and broccoli on the basket. Cover the pot.
3. Set it to pressure. Cook at high pressure for 2 minutes.
4. Release the pressure quickly. Crack the eggs into a bowl and beat.
5. Season with salt, pepper, parsley, and thyme. Put the vegetables on a small baking pan. Layer with the cheese and pour in the beaten eggs Place on the basket.
6. Choose air crisp function. Seal the crisping lid. Cook at 350 degrees for 20 minutes.

Nutrition: Calories 400, Total Fat 28g, Saturated Fat 16.5g, Cholesterol 242mg, Sodium 688mg, Total Carbohydrate 12.8g, Dietary Fiber 3.3g, Total Sugars 5.8g, Protein 26.2g, Potassium 537mg

Bacon & Scrambled Eggs

Preparation time: 15 minutes

Cooking Time: 20 minutes

Servings: 2

Ingredients:

- 4 strips bacon
- 2 eggs
- 1 tablespoon milk

- Salt and pepper to taste

Directions:

1. Place the bacon inside. Set it to air crisp.
2. Cover the crisping lid. Cook at 390 degrees for 3 minutes.
3. Flip the bacon and cook for another 2 minutes. Remove the bacon and set it aside.
4. Whisk the eggs and milk in a bowl. Season with salt and pepper.
5. Set to sauté. Add the eggs and cook until firm.

Nutrition: Calories 272, Total Fat 20.4g, Saturated Fat 6.7g, Cholesterol 206mg, Sodium 943mg, Total Carbohydrate 1.3g, Dietary Fiber 0g, Total Sugars 0.7g, Protein 19.9g, Potassium 279mg

French toast

Preparation time: 15 minutes

Cooking Time: 20 minutes

Servings: 2

Ingredients:

- 2 eggs, beaten
- 1/4 cup milk
- 1/4 cup brown sugar
- 1 tablespoon honey
- 1 teaspoon cinnamon
- 1/4 teaspoon nutmeg
- 4 slices wholemeal bread, sliced into strips

Directions:

1. In a bowl, combine all the ingredients except the bread. Mix well.
2. Dip each strip in the mixture. Place the bread strips on the basket.
3. Place the basket inside the pot. Cover with the crisping lid. Set it to air crisp.
4. Cook at 320 degrees for 10 minutes.

Nutrition: Calories 295, Total Fat 6.1g, Saturated Fat 2.1g, Cholesterol 166mg, Sodium 332mg, Total Carbohydrate 49.8g, Dietary Fiber 3.9g, Total Sugars 29.4g, Protein 11.9g, Potassium 112mg

Eggs & Veggie Burrito

Preparation time: 30 minutes

Cooking Time: 35 minutes

Servings: 8

Ingredients:

- 3 eggs, beaten
- Salt and pepper to taste
- Cooking spray
- 8 tortillas
- 2 red bell peppers, sliced into strips
- 1 onion, sliced thinly

Directions:

1. Beat the eggs in a bowl. Season with salt and pepper. Set aside.
2. Choose to sauté mode. Spray with the oil. Cook the vegetables until soft. Remove and set aside. Pour the eggs into the pot. Cook until firm.
3. Wrap the eggs and veggies with a tortilla.

Nutrition: Calories 92, Total Fat 2.5g, Saturated Fat 0.6g, Cholesterol 61mg, Sodium 35mg, Total Carbohydrate 14.4g, Dietary Fiber 2.2g, Total Sugars 2.4g, Protein 3.9g, Potassium 143mg

Breakfast Casserole

Preparation time: 50 minutes

Cooking Time: 55 minutes

Servings: 4

Ingredients:

- Cooking spray
- 1 lb. hash browns
- 1 lb. breakfast sausage, cooked and crumbled
- 1 red bell pepper, diced
- 1 green bell pepper, diced
- 1 onion, diced
- 4 eggs
- Salt and pepper to taste

Directions:

1. Coat a small baking pan with oil. Place the hash browns on the bottom part.
2. Add the sausage, and then the onion and bell peppers.
3. Place the pan on top of the basket. Put the basket inside the pot.
4. Close the crisping lid. Set it to air crisp. Cook at 350 degrees F for 10 minutes.
5. Open the lid. Crack the eggs on top. Cook for another 10 minutes.
6. Season with salt and pepper.

Nutrition: Calories 513 Total Fat 34g Saturated Fat 9.3g Cholesterol 173mg Sodium 867mg Total Carbohydrate 30g Dietary Fiber 3.1g Total Sugars 3.1g Protein 21.1g Potassium 761mg

Herb & Cheese Frittata

Preparation time: 25 minutes

Cooking Time: 30 minutes

Servings: 4

Ingredients:

- 4 eggs
- 1/2 cup half and half
- 2 tablespoons parsley, chopped
- 2 tablespoons chives, chopped
- 1/4 cup shredded cheddar cheese
- Salt and pepper to taste

Directions:

1. Beat the eggs in a bowl. Add the rest of the ingredients and stir well.
2. Pour the mixture into a small baking pan.
3. Place the pan on top of the basket.
4. Seal the crisping lid. Set it to air crisp. Cook at 330 degrees F for 15 minutes.

Nutrition: Calories 132 Total Fat 10.2g Saturated Fat 5g Cholesterol 182mg Sodium 119mg Total Carbohydrate 1.9g Dietary Fiber 0.1g Total Sugars 0.5g Protein 8.3g Potassium 121mg

Roasted Garlic Potatoes

Preparation time: 30 minutes

Cooking Time: 35 minutes

Servings: 6

Ingredients:

- 2 lb. baby potatoes, sliced into wedges
- 2 tablespoons olive oil
- 2 teaspoons garlic salt

Directions: Toss the potatoes in olive oil and garlic salt. Add the potatoes to the basket. Seal the crisping lid. Set it to air crisp. Cook at 390 degrees F for 20 minutes.

Nutrition: Calories 131Total Fat 4.8g Saturated Fat 0.7g Cholesterol 0mg Sodium 15mg Total Carbohydrate 19.5g Dietary Fiber 3.9g Total Sugars 0.2g Protein 4.1g Potassium 635mg

Tofu Scramble

Preparation time: 30 minutes

Cooking Time: 35 minutes

Servings: 4

Ingredients:

- 2 tablespoons olive oil, divided
- 2 tablespoons soy sauce
- 1/2 cup onion, chopped
- 1 teaspoon turmeric
- 1/2 teaspoon onion powder
- 1/2 teaspoon garlic powder
- 1 block firm tofu, sliced into cubes

Directions:

1. Mix all the ingredients except the tofu. Soak the tofu in the mixture.
2. Place the tofu in the pot. Seal the pot. Cover with the crisping lid.
3. Cook at 370 degrees F for 15 minutes.

Nutrition: Calories 90 Total Fat 8g Saturated Fat 1.2g Cholesterol 0mg Sodium 455mg Total Carbohydrate 3.2g Dietary Fiber 0.7g Total Sugars 1.1g Protein 2.7g Potassium 93mg

Avocado Egg

Preparation time: 30 minutes

Cooking Time: 35 minutes

Servings: 2

Ingredients:

- 1 avocado, sliced in half and pitted
- 2 eggs
- Salt and pepper to taste
- 1/4 cup cheddar, shredded

Directions:

1. Crack the egg into the avocado slice. Season with salt and pepper.
2. Put it on the basket. Seal the crisping lid.
3. Set it to air crisp. Cook at 400 degrees F for 15 minutes.
4. Sprinkle with the cheese 3 minutes before it is cooked.

Nutrition: Calories 281Total Fat 23g Saturated Fat 6g Cholesterol 178mg Sodium 158mg Total

Carbohydrates 9g Dietary Fiber 6g Protein 11g Potassium 548mg

Coconut French toast

Preparation Time: 10 minutes
Cooking Time: 16 minutes

Servings: 5

Ingredients:

- 1/4 cup milk
- 3 large eggs
- 1 (12-oz. loaf bread- 10 slices
- 1/4 cup sugar
- Cooking spray
- 1 cup of coconut milk
- 10 (1/4-inch-thick slices pineapple, peeled
- 1/2 cup coconut flakes

Directions:

1. Whisk the coconut milk with sugar, eggs, and fat-free milk in a bowl.
2. Dip the bread in this mixture and keep it aside for 1 minute.
3. Prepare and preheat the Ninja Foodi Grill on a medium-temperature setting.
4. Once it is preheated, open the lid and place 5 bread slices on the grill.
5. Cover the Ninja Foodi Grill's lid and let it grill on the "Grilling Mode" for 2 minutes.
6. Flip the slices and continue grilling for another 2 minutes.
7. Cook the remaining 5 slices in a similar way.
8. Now grill 5 pineapple slices on the grill for 2 minutes per side.
9. Grill the remaining pineapple in the same way.

10. Serve the bread with pineapple on top.
11. Garnish with coconut and serve.

Nutrition: Calories: 197, Total Fat: 15.4 g, Saturated Fat: 4.2 g, Cholesterol: 168 mg, Sodium: 203 mg, Total Carbs: 58.5 g, Sugar: 1.1 g, Fiber: 4 g, Protein: 7.9 g

Banana Bread

Preparation Time: 10 minutes

Cooking Time: 50 minutes

Servings: 8

Ingredients:

- 2 cups flour
- 1 teaspoon baking powder
- ½ cup sugar
- ½ cup butter, softened
- 2 eggs
- 1 tablespoon vanilla extract
- 4 bananas, peeled and mashed

Directions:

1. Grease a 7-inch springform pan.
2. In a bowl, mix flour and baking powder.
3. In another bowl, add sugar, butter, and eggs and beat until creamy.
4. Add the bananas and vanilla extract and beat until well combined.
5. Slowly add flour mixture, 1 cup at a time, and mix until smooth.
6. Place mixture into prepared loaf pan evenly.
7. In the pot of Ninja Foodi, place 1 cup of water.
8. Arrange the "Reversible Rack" in the pot of Ninja Foodi.
9. Place the pan over the "Reversible Rack."
10. Close the Ninja Foodi with the pressure lid and place the pressure valve in "Seal" position.
11. Select "Pressure" and set it to "High" for 50 minutes.

12. Press "Start/Stop" to begin cooking.
13. Switch the valve to "Vent" and do a "Quick" release.
14. Open the lid place the pan onto a wire rack to cool for about 10 minutes.
15. Carefully invert bread onto the wire rack to cool completely.
16. Cut into desired sized slices and serve.

Nutrition: Calories: 336, Fat: 13.1 g, Saturated Fat: 7.8 g, Carbohydrates: 50.4 g, Fiber 2.4 g, Sodium 99 mg, Protein: 5.4 g

Dried Fruit Oatmeal

Preparation Time: 10 minutes

Cooking Time: 8 hours

Servings: 8

Ingredients:

- 2 cups steel-cut oats
- 1/3 cup dried apricots, chopped
- 1/3 cup raisins
- 1/3 cup dried cherries
- 1 teaspoon ground cinnamon
- 4 cups milk
- 4 cups water
- ¼ teaspoon liquid stevia

Directions:

1. In the pot of Ninja Foodie, place all ingredients and stir to combine.
2. Close the Ninja Foodi with a crisping lid and select "Slow Cooker."
3. Set on "Low" for 6-8 hours.
4. Press "Start/Stop" to begin cooking.
5. Open the lid and serve warm.

Nutrition: Calories: 148, Fat: 3.5g, Saturated Fat: 1.7 g, Trans Fat:1.8g, Carbohydrates: 24.2 g, Fiber 3.2 g, Sodium 67 mg, Protein: 5.9 g

Eggs in Avocado Cups

Preparation Time: 10 minutes

Cooking Time: 12 minutes

Servings: 2

Ingredients:

- 1 avocado, halved and pitted
- Salt and ground black pepper, as required
- 2 eggs
- 1 tablespoon Parmesan cheese, shredded
- 1 teaspoon fresh chives, minced

Directions:

1. Arrange a greased square piece of foil in "Cook & Crisp Basket."
2. Arrange the "Cook & Crisp Basket" in the pot of Ninja Foodi.
3. Close the Ninja Foodi with a crisping lid and select "Bake/Roast."
4. Set the temperature to 390 degrees F for 5 minutes.
5. Press "Start/Stop" to begin preheating.
6. Carefully scoop out about 2 teaspoons of flesh from each avocado half.
7. Crack 1 egg in each avocado half and sprinkle with salt, black pepper, and cheese.
8. After preheating, open the lid.
9. Place the avocado halves into the "Cook & Crisp Basket."
10. Close the Ninja Foodi with a crisping lid and Select "Bake/Roast."
11. Set the temperature to 390 degrees F for 12 minutes.
12. Press "Start/Stop" to begin cooking.
13. Open the lid and transfer the avocado halves onto serving plates.
14. Top with Parmesan and chives and serve.

Nutrition: Calories: 278, Fat: 24.7 g, Saturated Fat: 5.9 g, Trans Fat:18.8g, Carbohydrates: 9.1 g, Fiber 6.7 g, Sodium 188 mg, Protein: 8.4 g

Chicken Omelet

Preparation Time: 10 minutes

Cooking Time: 16 minutes

Servings: 2

Ingredients:

- 1 teaspoon butter
- 1 small yellow onion, chopped
- ½ jalapeño pepper, seeded and chopped
- 3 eggs
- Salt and ground black pepper, as required
- ¼ cup cooked chicken, shredded

Directions:

1. Select the "Sauté/Sear" setting of Ninja Foodi and place the butter into the pot.
2. Press "Start/Stop" to begin cooking and heat for about 2-3 minutes.
3. Add the onion and cook for about 4-5 minutes.
4. Add the jalapeño pepper and cook for about 1 minute.
5. Meanwhile, in a bowl, add the eggs, salt, and black pepper and beat well.
6. Press "Start/Stop" to stop cooking and stir in the chicken.
7. Top with the egg mixture evenly.
8. Close the Ninja Foodi with a crisping lid and select "Air Crisp."
9. Set the temperature to 355 degrees F for 5 minutes.
10. Press "Start/Stop" to begin cooking.
11. Open the lid and transfer the omelet onto a plate.
12. Cut into equal-sized wedges and serve hot.

Nutrition: Calories: 153, Fat: 9.1 g, Saturated Fat: 3.4 g, Carbohydrates: 4 g, Fiber 0.9 g, Sodium 196 mg, Protein: 13.8 g

Sausage & Bell Pepper Frittata

Preparation Time: 15 minutes

Cooking Time: 18 minutes

Servings: 2

Ingredients:

- 1 tablespoon olive oil
- 1 chorizo sausage, sliced
- 1½ cups bell peppers, seeded and chopped
- 4 large eggs
- Salt and ground black pepper, as required
- 2 tablespoons feta cheese, crumbled
- 1 tablespoon fresh parsley, chopped

Directions:

1. Select the "Sauté/Sear" setting of Ninja Foodi and place the butter into the pot.
2. Press "Start/Stop" to begin cooking and heat for about 2-3 minutes.
3. Add the sausage and bell peppers and cook for 6-8 minutes or until golden brown.
4. Meanwhile, in a small bowl, add the eggs, salt, and black pepper and beat well.
5. Press "Start/Stop" to stop cooking and place the eggs over the sausage mixture, followed by the cheese and parsley.
6. Close the Ninja Foodi with a crisping lid and select "Air Crisp."
7. Set the temperature to 355 degrees F for 10 minutes.
8. Press "Start/Stop" to begin cooking.
9. Open the lid and transfer the frittata onto a platter.
10. Cut into equal-sized wedges and serve hot.

Nutrition: Calories: 398, Fat: 31 g, Saturated Fat: 9.3 g, Carbohydrates: 8 g, Fiber 1.3 g, Sodium 636 mg, Protein: 22.9 g

Eggs with Tomatoes

Preparation Time: 15 minutes

Cooking Time: 8 hours

Servings: 6

Ingredients:

- 1 tablespoon olive oil
- 1 medium yellow onion, chopped
- 2 garlic cloves, minced
- 1 jalapeño pepper, seeded and chopped finely
- 2 teaspoons smoked paprika
- 1 teaspoon ground cumin
- Salt, as required
- 1 (26-ounce) can diced tomatoes
- 6 eggs
- ¼ cup feta cheese, crumbled

Directions:

1. Select the "Sauté/Sear" setting of Ninja Foodi and place the butter into the pot.
2. Press "Start/Stop" to begin cooking and heat for about 2-3 minutes.
3. Add the onion and cook for about 3-4 minutes.
4. Add the garlic, jalapeño, paprika, cumin, and salt and cook for about 1 minute.
5. Press "Start/Stop" to stop cooking.
6. Close the Ninja Foodi with a crisping lid and select "Slow Cooker."
7. Set on "Low" for 8 hours.
8. Press "Start/Stop" to begin cooking.
9. Open the lid and with the back of a spoon, make 6 wells in the tomato mixture.
10. Carefully crack 1 egg in each well.
11. Close the Ninja Foodi with a crisping lid and select "Slow Cooker."
12. Set on "High" for 20 minutes.
13. Press "Start/Stop" to begin cooking.
14. Open the lid and serve hot with the topping of cheese.

Nutrition: Calories: 134, Fat: 8.5 g, Saturated Fat: 2.7 g, Carbohydrates: 8.1g, Fiber 2.3 g, Sodium 166 mg, Protein: 8 g

Grilled French toast

Preparation Time: 10 minutes

Cooking Time: 8 minutes

Servings: 3

Ingredients:

- 3- 1-inch slices challah bread
- 2 eggs
- Juice of ½ orange
- ½ quart strawberries, quartered
- 1-tablespoon honey
- 1-tablespoon balsamic vinegar
- 1-teaspoon orange zest
- 1/2 sprig fresh rosemary
- ½-teaspoon vanilla extract
- Salt to taste
- 1/4 cup heavy cream
- Fine sugar, for dusting, optional

Directions:

1. Spread a foil sheet on a working surface.
2. Add strawberries, balsamic, orange juice, rosemary, and zest.
3. Fold the foil edges to make a pocket.
4. Whisk egg with cream, honey, vanilla, and a pinch of salt.
5. Dip and soak the bread slices in this mixture and shake off the excess.
6. Prepare and preheat the Ninja Foodi Grill in the medium-temperature setting.
7. Once it is preheated, open the lid and place the bread slices and the foil packet on the grill.
8. Cover the Ninja Foodi Grill's lid and let them grill on the "Grilling Mode" for 2 minutes in batches.
9. Flip the bread slices and continue grilling for another 2 minutes.
10. Serve the bread with the strawberry mix on top.

Nutrition: Calories: 387, Total Fat: 6 g, Saturated Fat: 9.9 g, Cholesterol: 41 mg, Sodium: 154 mg, Total Carbs: 37.4 g, Fiber: 2.9 g, Sugar: 15.3 g, Protein: 14.6 g

Quinoa Porridge

Preparation Time: 10 minute

Cooking Time: 1 minutes

Servings: 6

Ingredients:

- 1¼ cups water
- 1 cup fresh apple juice
- 1½ cups uncooked quinoa, rinsed
- 1 tablespoon honey
- 1 cinnamon stick
- Pinch of salt

Directions:

1. In the pot of Ninja Foodi, add all ingredients and stir to combine well.
2. Close the Ninja Foodi with the pressure lid and place the pressure valve in the "Seal" position.
3. Select "Pressure" and set it to "High" for 1 minute.
4. Press "Start/Stop" to begin cooking.
5. Switch the valve to "Vent" and do a "Quick" release.
6. Open the lid, and with a fork, fluff the quinoa.
7. Serve warm.

Nutrition: Calories: 186, Fat: 2.6 g, Saturated Fat: 0.3 g, Trans Fat:2.3g, Carbohydrates: 34.8 g, Fiber 3.1 g, Sodium 31 mg, Protein: 6 g

Sausage with Eggs

Preparation Time: 10 minutes
Cooking Time: 10 minutes

Servings: 4

Ingredients:

- 4 sausage links
- 2 cups chopped kale
- 1 medium sweet yellow onion
- 4 eggs
- 1-cup mushrooms - Olive oil

Directions:

1. Prepare and preheat the Ninja Foodi Grill in a High-temperature setting.
2. Once it is preheated, open the lid and place the sausages on the grill. Cover the Ninja Foodi Grill's lid and let it grill on the "Grilling Mode" for 2 minutes.
3. Flip the sausages and continue grilling for another 3 minutes
4. Now spread the onion, mushrooms, and kale in an iron skillet.
5. Crack the eggs in between the sausages.
6. Bake this mixture for 5 minutes in the oven at 350 degrees F.
7. Serve warm and fresh.

Nutrition: Calories: 212, Total Fat: 11.8 g, Saturated Fat: 2.2 g, Cholesterol: 23mg, Sodium: 321 mg, Total Carbs: 14.6 g, Dietary Fiber: 4.4 g, Sugar: 8 g, Protein: 17.3 g

Espresso Glazed Bagels

Preparation Time: 10 minutes
Cooking Time: 8 minutes

Servings: 4

Ingredients:

- 4 bagels split in half
- 1/4 cup coconut milk
- 1-cup fine sugar
- 2 tablespoons black coffee
- 2 tablespoons coconut flakes

Directions:

1. Prepare and preheat the Ninja Foodi Grill on a medium-temperature setting.
2. Once it is preheated, open the lid and place 2 bagels in the grill.
3. Cover the Ninja Foodi Grill's lid and let it grill on the "Grilling Mode" for 2 minutes.
4. Flip the bagel and continue grilling for another 2 minutes.
5. Grill the remaining bagels in a similar way.
6. Whisk the rest of the ingredients in a bowl well.
7. Drizzle this sauce over the grilled bagels.
8. Serve.

Nutrition: Calories: 412, Total Fat: 24.8 g, Saturated Fat: 12.4 g, Cholesterol: 3 mg, Sodium: 132 mg, Total Carbs: 43.8 g, Dietary Fiber: 3.9 g, Sugar: 2.5 g, Protein: 18.9 g

Oats Granola

Preparation Time: 15 minutes

Cooking Time: 2 hours 30 minutes

Servings: 16

Ingredients:

- ½ cup sunflower kernels
- 5 cups rolled oats
- 2 tablespoons ground flax seeds
- ¾ cup applesauce
- ¼ cup olive oil
- ¼ cup unsalted butter

- 1 teaspoon ground cinnamon
- ½ cup dates pitted and chopped finely
- ½ cup golden raisins

Directions:

1. Grease the pot of Ninja Foodie.
2. In the greased pot of Ninja Foodie, add sunflower kernels, rolled oats, flax seeds, applesauce, oil, butter, and cinnamon, and stir to combine.
3. Close the Ninja Foodi with a crisping lid and select "Slow Cooker."
4. Set on "High" for 2½ hours.
5. Press "Start/Stop" to begin cooking.
6. Stir the mixture after every 30 minutes.
7. Open the lid and transfer the granola onto a large baking sheet.
8. Add the dates and raisins and stir to combine.
9. Set aside to cool completely before serving.
10. You can preserve this granola in an airtight container.

Nutrition: Calories:189, Fat: 10 g, Saturated Fat: 2.8 g , Trans Fat:7.2g, Carbohydrates: 27.7 g, Fiber:4g, Sodium 3mg, Protein: 4.6 g

Spinach & Turkey Cups

Preparation Time: 15 minutes

Cooking Time: 23 minutes

Servings: 3

Ingredients:

- 1 tablespoon unsalted butter
- 1 pound fresh baby spinach
- 4 eggs
- 7 ounces cooked turkey, chopped
- 4 teaspoons unsweetened almond milk
- Salt and ground black pepper, as required

Directions:

1. Select the "Sauté/Sear" setting of Ninja Foodi and place the butter into the pot.
2. Press "Start/Stop" to begin cooking and heat for about 2-3 minutes.
3. Add the spinach and cook for about 2-3 minutes or until just wilted.
4. Press "Start/Stop" to stop cooking and drain the liquid completely.
5. Transfer the spinach into a bowl and set aside to cool slightly.
6. Arrange the "Cook & Crisp Basket" in the pot of Ninja Foodi.
7. Close the Ninja Foodi with a crisping lid and select "Air Crisp."
8. Set the temperature to 355 degrees F for 5 minutes.
9. Press "Start/Stop" to begin preheating.
10. Divide the spinach into 4 greased ramekins, followed by the turkey.
11. Crack 1 egg into each ramekin and drizzle with almond milk.
12. Sprinkle with salt and black pepper.
13. After preheating, open the lid.
14. Place the ramekins into the "Cook & Crisp Basket."
15. Close the Ninja Foodi with a crisping lid and select "Air Crisp."
16. Set the temperature to 355 degrees F for 20 minutes.
17. Press "Start/Stop" to begin cooking.
18. Open the lid and serve hot.

Nutrition: Calories: 200, Fat: 10.2 g, Saturated Fat: 4.1 g, Carbohydrates: 4.5 g, Fiber 2.5 g, Sodium 249 mg, Protein: 23.4 g

Bruschetta Portobello Mushrooms

Preparation Time: 10 minutes
Cooking Time: 8 minutes
Servings: 6

Ingredients:

- 2 cups cherry tomatoes cut in half
- 3 tablespoons red onion, diced
- 3 tablespoons fresh basil shredded
- Salt and black pepper to taste
- 4 tablespoons butter
- 1 teaspoon dried oregano
- 6 large Portobello Mushrooms, caps only, washed and dried
- For Balsamic glaze:
- 2 teaspoons brown sugar
- 1/4 cup balsamic vinegar

Directions:

1. Start by preparing the balsamic glaze and take all its ingredients in a saucepan.
2. Stir cook this mixture for 8 minutes on medium heat then remove from the heat.
3. Take the mushrooms and brush them with the prepared glaze.
4. Stuff the remaining ingredients into the mushrooms.
5. Prepare and preheat the Ninja Foodi Grill in the medium-temperature setting.
6. Once it is preheated, open the lid and place the stuffed mushrooms in the grill with their cap side down.
7. Cover the Ninja Foodi Grill's lid and let it grill on the "Grilling Mode" for 8 minutes.
8. Serve.

Nutrition: Calories: 331: Total Fat: 2.5 g: Saturated Fat: 0.5 g: Cholesterol: 35 mg, Sodium: 595 mg, Total Carbs: 69 g, Fiber: 12.2 g, Sugar: 12.5 g, Protein: 8.7g

Sausage Mixed Grill

Preparation Time: 5 minutes
Cooking Time: 22 minutes

Servings: 4

Ingredients:

- 8 mini bell peppers
- 2 heads radicchio, each cut into 6 wedges
- Canola oil, for brushing
- Sea salt
- Freshly ground black pepper
- 6 breakfast sausage links
- 6 hot or sweet Italian sausage links

Directions:

1. Insert the grill grate and close the hood. Select grill set the temperature to max and set the time to 22 minutes. Select start
2. Stop to begin preheating.
3. While the unit is preheating, brush the bell peppers and radicchio with the oil. Season with salt and black pepper.
4. When the unit beeps to signify it has preheated, place the bell peppers and radicchio on the grill grate close the hood, and cook for 10 minutes, without flipping.
5. Meanwhile, poke the sausages with a fork or knife and brush them with some of the oil.
6. After 10 minutes, remove the vegetables and set them aside. Decrease the temperature to low. Place the sausages on the grill grate close the hood and cook for 6 minutes.
7. Flip the sausages. Close the hood and cook for 6 minutes more. Remove the sausages from the grill grate.
8. Serve the sausages and vegetables on a large cutting board or serving tray.

Nutrition: Calories: 473, Fat: 34g, Saturated Fat: 11g, Cholesterol: 73mg, Sodium: 1051mg, Carbohydrates: 14g, Fiber: 2g, Protein: 28g

Sausage and Egg Loaded Breakfast Pockets

Preparation Time: 15 minutes
Cooking Time: 23 minutes
Servings: 4

Ingredients:

- 1 (6-ounce) package ground breakfast sausage, crumbled
- 3 large eggs, lightly beaten
- 1/3 cup diced red bell pepper
- 1/3 cup thinly sliced scallions (green part only)
- Sea salt
- Freshly ground black pepper
- 1 (16-ounce) package pizza dough
- All-purpose flour, for dusting
- 1 cup shredded cheddar cheese
- 2 tablespoons canola oil

Directions:

1. Select roast, set the temperature to 375°f, and set the time to 15 minutes. Select start
2. Stop to begin preheating.
3. When the unit beeps to signify it has preheated, place the sausage directly in the pot.
4. Close the hood, and cook for 10 minutes, checking the sausage every 2 to 3 minutes, breaking apart larger pieces with a wooden spoon.
5. After 10 minute, pour the eggs, bell pepper, and scallions into the pot.
6. Stir to incorporate with the sausage evenly.
7. Close the hood and let the eggs cook for the remaining 5 minutes, stirring occasionally.
8. Transfer the sausage and egg mixture to a medium bowl to cool slightly. Season with salt and pepper.
9. Insert the crisper basket and close the hood.
10. Select air crisp, set the temperature to 350°f, and set the time to 8 minutes. Select start
11. Stop to begin preheating.
12. Meanwhile, divide the dough into four equal pieces.
13. Lightly dust a clean work surface with flour. Roll each piece of dough into a 5-inch round of even thickness.
14. Divide the sausage-egg mixture and cheese evenly among each round. Brush the outside edge of the dough with water.
15. Fold the dough over the filling, forming a half circle. Pinch the edges of the dough together to seal in the filling. Brush both sides of each pocket with the oil.
16. When the unit beeps to signify it has preheated, place the breakfast pockets in the basket. Close the hood and cook for 6 to 8 minutes, or until golden brown.

Nutrition: Calories: 639, Fat: 40g, Saturated Fat: 8g, Cholesterol: 169mg, Sodium: 765mg, Carbohydrates: 50g, Fiber: 4g, Protein: 24g

Appetizers and Snacks

Watermelon Jerky

Preparation Time: 5 minutes

Cooking Time: 12 Hours

Servings: ½ Cup

Ingredients:

- 1 cup seedless watermelon (1-inch) cubes

Directions:

1. Arrange the watermelon cubes in a single layer in the Cook & Crisp Basket. Place the basket in the pot and close the Crisping Lid.
2. Press Dehydrate, set the temperature to 135°F and set the time to 12 hours. Select Start/Stop to begin.
3. When dehydrating is complete, remove the basket from the pot and transfer the jerky to an airtight container.

Nutrition Calories: 46; Total fat: 0g; Saturated fat: 0g; Cholesterol: 0mg; Sodium: 6mg; Carbohydrates: 12g; Fiber: 1g; Protein: 1g

Dried Mango

Preparation Time: 5 minutes

Cooking Time: 8 Hours

Servings: 2

Ingredients:

- ½ mango, peeled, pitted, and cut into 3/8-inch slices

Directions:

1. Arrange the mango slices flat in a single layer in the Cook & Crisp Basket. Place in the pot and close the Crisping Lid.

2. Press Dehydrate, set the temperature to 135°F and set the time to 8 hours. Select Start/Stop to begin.
3. When dehydrating is complete, remove the basket from the pot and transfer the mango slices to an airtight container.

Nutrition Calories: 67; Total fat: 0g; Saturated fat: 0g; Cholesterol: 0mg; Sodium: 2mg; Carbohydrates: 18g; Fiber: 2g; Protein: 1g

Beet Chips

Preparation Time: 5 minutes

Cooking Time: 8 Hours

Servings: ½ Cup

Ingredients:

- ½ beet, peeled and cut into 1/8-inch slices

Directions:

1. Arrange the beet slices flat in a single layer in the Cook & Crisp Basket. Place in the pot and close the Crisping Lid.
2. Press Dehydrate, set the temperature to 135°F and set the time to 8 hours. Select Start/Stop to begin.
3. When dehydrating is complete, remove the basket from the pot and transfer the beet chips to an airtight container.

Nutrition: Calories: 35; Total fat: 0g; Saturated fat: 0g; Cholesterol: 0mg; Sodium: 64mg; Carbohydrates: 8g; Fiber: 2g; Protein: 1g

Maple Candied Bacon

Preparation Time: 5 minutes

Cooking Time: 40 Minutes

Servings: 12

Ingredients:

- ½ cup maple syrup
- ¼ cup brown sugar
- Nonstick cooking spray
- 1 pound (12 slices) thick-cut bacon

Directions:

1. Place the Reversible Rack in the pot. Close the Crisping Lid. Preheat the unit by selecting Air Crisp, setting the temperature to 400°F, and setting the time to 5 minutes.
2. Meanwhile, in a small mixing bowl, mix the maple syrup and brown sugar.
3. Once it has preheated, carefully line the Reversible Rack with aluminum foil. Spray the foil with cooking spray.
4. Arrange 4 to 6 slices of bacon on the rack in a single layer. Brush them with the maple syrup mixture.
5. Close the Crisping Lid. Select Air Crisp and set the temperature to 400°F. Set the time to 10 minutes, then select Start/Stop to begin.
6. After 10 minutes, flip the bacon and brush with more maple syrup mixture. Close the Crisping Lid, select Air Crisp, set the temperature to 400°F, and set the time to 10 minutes. Select Start/Stop to begin.
7. Cooking is complete when your desired crispiness is reached. Remove the bacon from the Reversible Rack and transfer to a cooling rack for 10 minutes. Repeat steps 4 through 6 with the remaining bacon.

Nutrition: (2 slices) Calories: 451; Total fat: 34g; Saturated fat: 11g; Cholesterol: 51mg; Sodium: 634mg; Carbohydrates: 27g; Fiber: 0g; Protein: 9g

Chili-Ranch Chicken Wings

Preparation Time: 10 minutes

Cooking Time: 28 Minutes

Servings: 4

Ingredients:

- ½ cup of water
- ½ cup hot pepper sauce
- 2 tablespoons unsalted butter, melted
- 1½ tablespoons apple cider vinegar
- 2 pounds frozen chicken wings
- ½ (1-ounce) envelope ranch salad dressing mix
- ½ teaspoon paprika
- Nonstick cooking spray

Directions:

1. Pour the water, hot pepper sauce, butter, and vinegar into the pot. Place the wings in the Cook & Crisp Basket and place the basket in the pot. Assemble the Pressure Lid, making sure the pressure release valve is in the Seal position.
2. Select Pressure and set it to High. Set the time to 5 minutes. Select Start/Stop to begin.
3. When pressure cooking is complete, quick release the pressure by turning the pressure release valve to the Vent position. Carefully remove the lid when the unit has finished releasing pressure.
4. Sprinkle the chicken wings with the dressing mix and paprika. Coat with cooking spray.
5. Close the Crisping Lid. Select Air Crisp, set the temperature to 375°F and set the time to 15 minutes. Select Start/Stop to begin.
6. After 7 minutes, open the Crisping Lid, then lift the basket and shake the wings. Coat with cooking spray. Lower the basket back into the pot and close the lid to resume cooking until the wings reach your desired crispiness.

Nutrition: Calories: 405; Total fat: 30g; Saturated fat: 10g; Cholesterol: 131mg; Sodium: 1782mg; Carbohydrates: 4g; Fiber: 0g; Protein: 28g

Crispy Cheesy Arancini

Preparation Time: 15 minutes

Cooking Time: 45 Minutes

Servings: 6

Ingredients:

- ½ cup extra-virgin olive oil, plus 1 tablespoon
- 1 small yellow onion, diced
- 2 garlic cloves, minced
- 5 cups chicken broth
- ½ cup white wine
- 2 cups arborio rice
- 1½ cups grated Parmesan cheese, plus more for garnish
- 1 cup frozen peas
- 1 teaspoon sea salt
- 1 teaspoon freshly ground black pepper
- 2 cups fresh breadcrumbs
- 2 large eggs

Directions:

1. Select Sear/Sauté and set it to Medium-High. Select Start/Stop to begin. Allow the pot to preheat for 5 minutes.
2. Add 1 tablespoon of oil and the onion to the preheated pot. Cook until soft and translucent, stirring occasionally. Add the garlic and cook for 1 minute.
3. Add the broth, wine, and rice to the pot; stir to incorporate. Assemble the Pressure Lid, making sure the pressure release valve is in the Seal position.
4. Select Pressure and set it to High. Set the time to 7 minutes. Press Start/Stop to begin.
5. When pressure cooking is complete, allow pressure to naturally release for 10 minutes, then quickly release any remaining pressure by turning the pressure release valve to the Vent position. Carefully remove the lid when

the unit has finished releasing pressure.

6. Add the Parmesan cheese, frozen peas, salt, and pepper. Stir vigorously until the rice begins to thicken. Transfer the risotto to a large mixing bowl and let cool.

7. Meanwhile, clean the pot. In a medium mixing bowl, stir together the bread crumbs and the remaining ½ cup of olive oil. In a separate mixing bowl, lightly beat the eggs.

8. Divide the risotto into 12 equal portions and form each one into a ball. Dip each risotto ball in the beaten eggs, then coat in the bread crumb mixture.

9. Arrange half of the arancini in the Cook & Crisp™ Basket in a single layer.

10. Close the Crisping Lid. Select Air Crisp, set the temperature to 400°F and set the time to 10 minutes. Select Start/Stop to begin.

11. Repeat steps 9 and 10 to cook the remaining arancini.

Nutrition: Calories: 769; Total fat: 32g; Saturated fat: 9g; Cholesterol: 98mg; Sodium: 1348mg; Carbohydrates: 91g; Fiber: 5g; Protein: 27g

Buffalo Chicken Meatballs

Preparation Time: 10 minutes

Cooking Time: 40 Minutes

Servings: 6

Ingredients:

- 1-pound ground chicken
- 1 carrot, minced
- 2 celery stalks, minced
- ¼ cup crumbled blue cheese
- ¼ cup buffalo sauce
- ¼ cup bread crumbs
- 1 egg
- 2 tablespoons extra-virgin olive oil
- ½ cup of water

Directions:

1. Select Sear/Sauté and set it to High. Select Start/Stop to begin. Allow the pot to preheat for 5 minutes.

2. Meanwhile, in a large mixing bowl, mix the chicken, carrot, celery, blue cheese, buffalo sauce, bread crumbs, and egg. Shape the mixture into 1½-inch meatballs.

3. Pour the olive oil into the preheated pot. Working in batches, place the meatballs in the pot and sear on all sides until browned. When each batch finishes cooking, transfer to a plate.

4. Place the Cook & Crisp Basket in the pot. Add the water, then place all the meatballs in the basket.

5. Assemble the Pressure Lid, making sure the pressure release valve is in the Seal position. Select Pressure and set to High. Set the time to 5 minutes. Select Start/Stop to begin.

6. When pressure cooking is complete, quick release the pressure by turning the pressure release valve to the Vent position. Carefully remove the lid when the unit has finished releasing pressure.

7. Close the Crisping Lid. Select Air Crisp, set the temperature to 360°F and set the time to 10 minutes. Select Start/Stop to begin.

8. After 5 minutes, open the lid, then lift the basket and shake the meatballs. Lower the basket back into the pot and close the lid to resume cooking until the meatballs achieve your desired crispiness.

Nutrition: Calories: 204; Total fat: 13g; Saturated fat: 4g; Cholesterol: 104mg; Sodium: 566mg; Carbohydrates: 5g; Fiber: 1g; Protein: 16g

Loaded Smashed Potatoes

Preparation Time: 10 minutes

Cooking Time: 30 Minutes

Servings: 4

Ingredients:

- 12 ounces baby Yukon Gold potatoes
- 1 teaspoon extra-virgin olive oil
- ¼ cup sour cream
- ¼ cup shredded Cheddar cheese
- 2 slices bacon, cooked and crumbled
- 1 tablespoon chopped fresh chives
- Sea salt

Directions:

1. Place the Cook & Crisp Basket in the pot. Close the Crisping Lid. Preheat the unit by selecting Air Crisp, setting the temperature to 350°F, and setting the time to 5 minutes. Press Start/Stop to begin.
2. Meanwhile, toss the potatoes with the oil until evenly coated.
3. Once the pot and basket are preheated, open the lid, and add the potatoes to the basket. Close the lid, select Air Crisp, set the temperature to 350°F and set the time to 30 minutes. Press Start/Stop to begin.
4. After 15 minutes, open the lid, then lift the basket and shake the potatoes. Lower the basket back into the pot and close the lid to resume cooking.
5. After 15 minutes, check the potatoes for your desired crispiness. They should be fork-tender.
6. Remove the potatoes from the basket. Use a large spoon to lightly crush the potatoes to split them. Top with sour cream, cheese, bacon, and chives, and season with salt.

Nutrition: Calories: 154; Total fat: 8g; Saturated fat: 4g; Cholesterol: 19mg; Sodium: 152mg; Carbohydrates: 16g; Fiber: 1g; Protein: 5g

Fried Pickles

Preparation Time: 10 minutes

Cooking Time: 10 Minutes

Servings: 4

Ingredients:

- 20 dill pickle slices
- ¼ cup all-purpose flour
- 1/8 teaspoon baking powder
- 3 tablespoons beer or seltzer water
- 1/8 teaspoon sea salt
- 2 tablespoons water, plus more if needed
- 2 tablespoons cornstarch
- 1½ cups panko breadcrumbs
- 1 teaspoon paprika
- 1 teaspoon garlic powder
- ¼ teaspoon cayenne pepper
- 2 tablespoons canola oil, divided

Directions:

1. Pat the pickle slices dry and place them on a dry plate in the freezer.
2. In a medium bowl, stir together the flour, baking powder, beer, salt, and water. The batter should be the consistency of cake batter. If it is too thick, add more water, 1 teaspoon at a time.
3. Place the cornstarch in a small shallow bowl.
4. In a separate large shallow bowl, combine the breadcrumbs, paprika, garlic powder, and cayenne pepper.
5. Remove the pickles from the freezer. Dredge each one in cornstarch. Tap off any excess, then coat in the batter. Lastly, coat evenly with the bread crumb mixture.
6. Insert the Crisper Basket and close the hood. Select AIR CRISP, set the temperature to 360°F, and set the time to 10 minutes. Select START/STOP to begin preheating.

7. When the unit beeps to signify it has preheated, place the breaded pickles in the basket, stacking them if necessary, and gently brush them with 1 tablespoon of oil. Close the hood and cook for 5 minutes
8. After 5 minutes, shake the basket and gently brush the pickles with the remaining 1 tablespoon of oil. Place the basket back in the unit and close the hood to resume cooking.
9. When cooking is complete, serve immediately.

Nutrition: Calories: 296; Total fat: 10g; Saturated fat: 1g; Cholesterol: 0mg; Sodium: 768mg; Carbohydrates: 44g; Fiber: 3g; Protein: 7g

Charred Shishito Peppers

Preparation Time: 5 minutes

Cooking Time: 10 Minutes

Servings: 4

Ingredients:

- 3 cups whole shishito peppers
- 2 tablespoons vegetable oil
- Flaky sea salt, for garnish

Directions:

1. Insert the Grill Grate and close the hood. Select GRILL, set the temperature to MAX, and set the time to 10 minutes. Select START/STOP to begin preheating.
2. While the unit is preheating, in a medium bowl, toss the peppers in the oil until evenly coated.
3. When the unit beeps to signify it has preheated, place the peppers on the Grill Grate. Gently press the peppers down to maximize grill marks. Close the hood and grill for 8 to 10 minutes, until they are blistered on all sides.

4. When cooking is complete, place the peppers in a serving dish and top with the flaky sea salt. Serve immediately.

Nutrition: Calories: 83; Total fat: 7g; Saturated fat: 1g; Cholesterol: 0mg; Sodium: 49mg; Carbohydrates: 5g; Fiber: 3g; Protein: 2g

Lemon-Garlic Artichokes

Preparation Time: 10 minutes

Cooking Time: 10 Minutes

Servings: 4

Ingredients:

- Juice of ½ lemon
- ½ cup canola oil
- 3 garlic cloves, chopped
- Sea salt
- Freshly ground black pepper
- 2 large artichokes, trimmed and halved

Directions:

1. Insert the Grill Grate and close the hood. Select GRILL, set the temperature to MAX, and set the time to 10 minutes. Select START/STOP to begin preheating.
2. While the unit is preheating, in a medium bowl, combine the lemon juice, oil, and garlic. Season with salt and pepper, then brush the artichoke halves with the lemon-garlic mixture.
3. When the unit beeps to signify it has preheated, place the artichokes on the Grill Grate, cut side down. Gently press them down to maximize grill marks. Close the hood and grill for 8 to 10 minutes, occasionally basting generously with the lemon-garlic mixture throughout cooking, until blistered on all sides.

Nutrition: Calories: 285; Total fat: 28g; Saturated fat: 2g; Cholesterol: 0mg; Sodium:

137mg; Carbohydrates: 10g; Fiber: 5g; Protein: 3g

Blistered Green Beans

Preparation Time: 5 minutes

Cooking Time: 10 Minutes

Servings: 4

Ingredients:

- 1-pound haricots verts or green beans, trimmed
- 2 tablespoons vegetable oil
- Juice of 1 lemon
- Pinch red pepper flakes
- Flaky sea salt
- Freshly ground black pepper

Directions:

1. Insert the Grill Grate and close the hood. Select GRILL, set the temperature to MAX, and set the time to 10 minutes. Select START/STOP to begin preheating.
2. While the unit is preheating, in a medium bowl, toss the green beans in oil until evenly coated.
3. When the unit beeps to signify it has preheated, place the green beans on the Grill Grate. Close the hood and grill for 8 to 10 minutes, tossing frequently until blistered on all sides.
4. When cooking is complete, place the green beans on a large serving platter. Squeeze lemon juice over the green beans, top with red pepper flakes, and season with sea salt and black pepper.

Nutrition: Calories: 100; Total fat: 7g; Saturated Fat: 1g; Cholesterol: 0mg; Sodium: 30mg; Carbohydrates: 10g; Fiber: 4g; Protein: 2g

Bacon Brussels Sprout

Preparation Time: 10 minutes

Cooking Time: 12 Minutes

Servings: 4

Ingredients:

- 1-pound Brussels sprouts, trimmed and halved
- 2 tablespoons extra-virgin olive oil
- 1 teaspoon sea salt
- ½ teaspoon freshly ground black pepper
- 6 slices bacon, chopped

Directions:

1. Insert the Crisper Basket and close the hood. Select AIR CRISP, set the temperature to 390°F, and set the time to 12 minutes. Select START/STOP to begin preheating.
2. Meanwhile, in a large bowl, toss the Brussels sprouts with olive oil, salt, pepper, and bacon.
3. When the unit beeps to signify it has preheated, add the Brussels sprouts to the basket. Close the hood and cook for 10 minutes.
4. After 6 minutes, shake the basket of Brussels sprouts. Place the basket back in the unit and close the hood to resume cooking.
5. After 6 minutes, check for desired crispness. Continue cooking up to 2 more minutes, if necessary.

Nutrition: Calories: 264; Total fat: 19g; Saturated fat: 5g; Cholesterol: 31mg; Sodium: 1155mg; Carbohydrates: 11g; Fiber: 4g; Protein: 15g

Grilled Asian-Style Broccoli

Preparation Time: 5 minutes

Cooking Time: 10 Minutes

Servings: 4

Ingredients:

- 4 tablespoons soy sauce
- 4 tablespoons balsamic vinegar
- 2 tablespoons canola oil
- 2 teaspoons maple syrup
- 2 heads broccoli, trimmed into florets
- Red pepper flakes, for garnish
- Sesame seeds, for garnish

Directions:

1. Insert the Grill Grate and close the hood. Select GRILL, set the temperature to MAX, and set the time to 10 minutes. Select START/STOP to begin preheating.
2. While the unit is preheating, in a large bowl, whisk together the soy sauce, balsamic vinegar, oil, and maple syrup. Add the broccoli and toss to coat evenly.
3. When the unit beeps to signify it has preheated, place the broccoli on the Grill Grate. Close the hood and grill for 8 to 10 minutes, until charred on all sides.
4. When cooking is complete, place the broccoli on a large serving platter. Garnish with red pepper flakes and sesame seeds. Serve immediately.

Nutrition: Calories: 133; Total fat: 8g; Saturated fat: 1g; Cholesterol: 0mg; Sodium: 948mg; Carbohydrates: 13g; Fiber: 4g; Protein: 5g

Honey-Glazed Grilled Carrots

Preparation Time: 10 minutes

Cooking Time: 10 Minutes

Servings: 4

Ingredients:

- 6 medium carrots, peeled and cut lengthwise
- 1 tablespoon canola oil
- 2 tablespoons unsalted butter, melted
- ¼ cup brown sugar, melted
- ¼ cup honey
- 1/8 teaspoon sea salt

Directions:

1. Insert the Grill Grate and close the hood. Select GRILL, set the temperature to MAX, and set the time to 10 minutes. Select START/STOP to begin preheating.
2. In a large bowl, toss the carrots and oil until well coated.
3. When the unit beeps to signify it has preheated, place carrots on the center of the Grill Grate. Close the hood and cook for 5 minutes.
4. Meanwhile, in a small bowl, whisk together the butter, brown sugar, honey, and salt.
5. After 5 minutes, open the hood and baste the carrots with the glaze. Using tongs, turn the carrots and baste the other side. Close the hood and cook for another 5 minutes.
6. When cooking is complete, serve immediately.

Nutrition: Calories: 218; Total fat: 9g; Saturated fat: 4g; Cholesterol: 15mg; Sodium: 119mg; Carbohydrates: 35g; Fiber: 2g; Protein: 1g

Garlicky Summer Squash and Charred Red Onion

Preparation Time: 15 minutes

Cooking Time: 15 Minutes

Servings: 4

Ingredients:

- ½ cup vegetable oil, plus 3 tablespoons
- ¼ cup white wine vinegar
- 1 garlic clove, grated
- 2 summer squash, sliced lengthwise about ¼-inch thick
- 1 red onion, peeled and cut into wedges
- Sea salt
- Freshly ground black pepper
- 1 (8-ounce) package crumbled feta cheese
- Red pepper flakes

Directions:

1. Insert the Grill Grate and close the hood. Select GRILL, set the temperature to MAX, and set the time to 15 minutes. Select START/STOP to begin preheating.
2. Meanwhile, in a small bowl, whisk together ½ cup oil, vinegar, and garlic, and set aside.
3. In a large bowl, toss the squash and onion with the remaining 3 tablespoons of oil until evenly coated. Season with salt and pepper.
4. When the unit beeps to signify it has preheated, arrange the squash and onions on the Grill Grate. Close the hood and cook for 6 minutes.
5. After 6 minutes, open the hood and flip the squash. Close the hood and cook for 6 to 9 minutes more.
6. When vegetables are cooked to the desired doneness, remove them from the grill. Arrange the vegetables on a large platter and top with the feta cheese. Drizzle the dressing over the top, and sprinkle with the red pepper flakes. Let stand for 15 minutes before serving.

Nutrition: Calories: 521; Total fat: 50g; Saturated fat: 16g; Cholesterol: 50mg; Sodium: 696mg; Carbohydrates: 11g; Fiber: 2g; Protein: 10g

Crispy Rosemary Potatoes

Preparation Time: 10 minutes

Cooking Time: 20 Minutes

Servings: 4

Ingredients:

- 2 pounds baby red potatoes, quartered
- 2 tablespoons extra-virgin olive oil
- ¼ cup dried onion flakes
- 1 teaspoon dried rosemary
- ½ teaspoon onion powder
- ½ teaspoon garlic powder
- ¼ teaspoon celery
- ¼ teaspoon freshly ground black pepper
- ½ teaspoon dried parsley
- ½ teaspoon sea salt

Directions:

1. Insert the Crisper Basket and close the hood. Select AIR CRISP, set the temperature to 390°F, and set the time to 20 minutes. Select START/STOP to begin preheating.
2. Meanwhile, place all the ingredients in a large bowl and toss until evenly coated.
3. When the unit beeps to signify it has preheated, add the potatoes to the basket. Close the hood and cook for 10 minutes.
4. After 10 minutes, shake the basket well. Place the basket back in the unit and close the hood to resume cooking.

5. After 10 minutes, check for desired crispness. Continue cooking up to 5 minutes more, if necessary.

Nutrition: Calories: 232; Total fat: 7g; Saturated fat: 1g; Cholesterol: 0mg; Sodium: 249mg; Carbohydrates: 39g; Fiber: 6g; Protein: 4g

Chicken Crisps

Preparation Time: 5-10 Minutes

Cooking Time: 8 Minutes

Servings: 4

Ingredients:

- ¼ teaspoon of sea salt
- ¼ teaspoon Black pepper (finely ground)
- ½ cup Italian seasoned breadcrumbs
- 2 tablespoons grated Parmesan cheese
- 1 boneless, skinless chicken breast, cut into 1-inch pieces
- ½ cup unsalted butter, melted

Directions:

1. In a mixing bowl, add the breadcrumbs, Parmesan cheese, salt, and black pepper. Combine the ingredients to mix well with each other.
2. Coat the chicken with the butter; coat them each with the crumb mixture.
3. Take Ninja Foodi multi-cooker, arrange it over a cooking platform, and open the top lid.
4. In the pot, arrange the Crisping Basket and coat with some cooking spray. In the basket, add the chicken breasts.
5. Seal the multi-cooker by locking it with the Crisping Lid; ensure to keep the pressure release valve locked/sealed.
6. Select the "AIR CRISP" mode and adjust the 390°F temperature level. Then, set the timer to 8 minutes and press "STOP/START"; it will start the

cooking process by building up inside pressure.
7. After 4 minutes, flip the breasts and continue cooking.
8. When the timer goes off, quickly release pressure by adjusting the pressure valve to the VENT. After pressure gets released, open the Crisping Lid. Serve warm.

Nutrition: Calories: 297 Fat: 22.5g Saturated Fat: 11g Trans Fat: 0g Carbohydrates: 7.5g Fiber: 0.5g Sodium: 315mg Protein: 10g

Appetizing Peppers

Preparation Time: 5-10 Minutes

Cooking Time: 12 Minutes

Servings: 4

Ingredients:

- 2 ounces tomato sauce
- 1 green onion, chopped
- 1 orange bell pepper, cut into strips
- 1 yellow bell pepper, cut into strips
- 2 tablespoons oregano, chopped
- Black pepper (ground) and salt to taste

Directions:

1. Take a multi-cooker, arrange it over a cooking platform, and open the top lid.
2. In the pot, add the ingredients and stir gently.
3. Seal the multi-cooker by locking it with the pressure lid, ensure to keep the pressure release valve locked/sealed.
4. Select the "PRESSURE" mode and select the "HI" pressure level. Then after, set the timer to 12 minutes and press "STOP/START," which will start the cooking process by building up inside pressure.
5. When the timer goes off, quickly release pressure by adjusting the pressure valve to the VENT. After

pressure gets released, open the pressure lid. Serve warm.

Nutrition: Calories: 54 Fat: 0g Saturated Fat: 0g Trans Fat: 0g Carbohydrates: 9g Fiber: 3g Sodium: 147mg Protein: 2g

Mayonnaise Corn

Preparation Time: 5-10 Minutes

Cooking Time: 14 Minutes

Servings: 3-4

Ingredients:

- ¼ cup sour cream
- ¼ cup mayonnaise
- 3 ears corn, husked, rinsed and dried
- Olive oil spray
- ½ teaspoon garlic powder
- ¼ teaspoon chili powder
- ¼ cup crumbled cotija cheese
- 1 teaspoon freshly squeezed lime juice
- Fresh cilantro leaves, for garnish
- ½ teaspoon salt
- ½ teaspoon Black pepper (ground)

Directions:

1. Take Ninja Foodi multi-cooker, arrange it over a cooking platform, and open the top lid.
2. In the pot, place the Crisping Basket and coat it with some cooking spray. In the basket, add the corn.
3. Seal the multi-cooker by locking it with the crisping lid, ensure to keep the pressure release valve locked/sealed.
4. Select the "AIR CRISP" mode and adjust the 400°F temperature level. Then, set the timer to 12 minutes and press "STOP/START," which will start the cooking process by building up inside pressure. Shake the basket after 6 minutes.
5. When the timer goes off, quickly release pressure by adjusting the pressure valve to the VENT. After

pressure gets released, open the Crisping Lid. Add the corn to a plate.
6. In a mixing bowl, stir together the sour cream, mayonnaise, cheese, lime juice, garlic powder, and chili powder.
7. Add the cream mixture over the corn. Season to taste with salt and black pepper. Top with cilantro, and more chili powder.

Nutrition: Calories: 265 Fat: 13.5g Saturated Fat: 5g Trans Fat: 0g Carbohydrates: 29g Fiber: 4g Sodium: 687mg Protein: 7.5g

Basil Shrimp Appetizer

Preparation Time: 5-10 Minutes

Cooking Time: 8 Minutes

Servings: 4-6

Ingredients:

- 2 teaspoons olive oil
- Black pepper (ground) and salt to taste
- 1-pound shrimp, peeled and deveined
- 1 tablespoon basil, chopped

Directions:

1. Take a multi-cooker, arrange it over a cooking platform, and open the top lid.
2. In the pot, place the Crisping Basket. In the basket, add all the ingredients and combine them.
3. Seal the multi-cooker by locking it with the crisping lid, ensure to keep the pressure release valve locked/sealed.
4. Select the "AIR CRISP" mode and adjust the 370°F temperature level. Then, set the timer to 8 minutes and press "STOP/START," which will start the cooking process by building up inside pressure.
5. When the timer goes off, quickly release pressure by adjusting the pressure valve to the VENT. After pressure gets released, open the Crisping Lid. Serve warm.

Nutrition: Calories: 117 Fat: 5g Saturated Fat: 1g Trans Fat: 0g Carbohydrates: 2g Fiber: 0g Sodium: 924mg Protein: 15g

Nutrition: Calories: 103 Fat: 1.5g Saturated Fat: 0g Trans Fat: 0g Carbohydrates: 11g Fiber: 3g Sodium: 411mg Protein: 3g

Seasoned Zucchini Chips

Preparation Time: 5-10 Minutes

Cooking Time: 10 Minutes

Servings: 5-6

Ingredients:

- 1 teaspoon Old Bay seasoning
- 1 teaspoon garlic salt
- ½ teaspoon kosher salt
- 1 large egg, beaten
- ¾ cup panko breadcrumbs
- 2 large zucchinis, cut into 1/4-inch rounds

Directions:

1. In a mixing bowl, beat the eggs. In another s bowl, combine the panko, seasoning, garlic salt, and kosher salt.
2. Evenly coat the zucchini rounds with the eggs and then with the panko.
3. Take a multi-cooker, arrange it over a cooking platform, and open the top lid.
4. In the pot, arrange the Crisping Basket. In the basket, add the zucchini rounds. Cook in batches if needed.
5. Seal the multi-cooker by locking it with the crisping lid; ensure to keep the pressure release valve locked/sealed.
6. Select the "AIR CRISP" mode and adjust the 350°F temperature level. Then, set the timer to 12 minutes and press "STOP/START"; which will start the cooking process by building up inside pressure.
7. When the timer goes off, quickly release pressure by adjusting the pressure valve to the VENT. After pressure gets released, open the Crisping Lid. Serve warm.

Maple Roasted Brussels sprouts with Bacon

Preparation Time: 10 Minutes

Cooking Time: 55 Minutes

Servings: 6

Ingredients:

- ¼ cup of extra-virgin olive oil
- 4 slices of bacon, to be cut into 1/2 – inch pieces
- ¼ teaspoon of freshly ground black pepper
- 1 pound of Brussels sprouts, to be trimmed
- 3 tablespoons of pure maple syrup
- ½ teaspoon of salt

Direction:

1. Preheat your oven to 400°F (200°C)
2. Put the Brussels sprouts in a single layer in a baking dish. Then drizzle with maple syrup, olive oil, and toss to coat. Sprinkle with bacon and season with black pepper and salt
3. Roast in the preheated oven until the bacon becomes crispy and the Brussels sprouts are caramelized in about 45 minutes; you will need to stir halfway through.

Nutrition: 175.3 calories Carbohydrates 13.6 grams 4% Protein 4.8 grams 10% Fat 12.1 grams 19% Cholesterol 6.6 mg 2% Sodium 352.2 mg 14%

Spicy Sweet Potato Chips

Preparation Time: 15 Minutes

Cooking Time: 30 Minutes

Servings: 6

Ingredients:

- 2 tablespoons of maple syrup
- 3 large, sweet potatoes, to be peeled and cut into 1/4- inch slices
- 2 tablespoons of olive oil
- ¼ teaspoon of cayenne pepper
- 1 pinch of salt and pepper to taste

Direction:

1. Preheat your oven to 450°F (230°C). Then line a baking sheet with aluminum foil.
2. Stir together maple syrup and cayenne pepper in a small bowl. Brush the sweet potato slices with the maple syrup and place them on the already prepared baking sheet. Add pepper and salt to taste.
3. Bake in the already preheated oven for 8 minutes and then turn the potato slices to the other side and brush with the leftover maple mixture and continue baking until it becomes tender in the middle and crispy edge about 7 minutes.

Nutrition: 252.6 calories Carbohydrates 50.2 grams 16% Protein 3.6 grams 7% Fat 4.6 grams 7% Sodium 125.6 mg 5%

Red Onion Marmalade

Preparation Time: 10 Minutes

Cooking Time: 30 Minutes

Cooking Time: 40 Minutes

Servings: 8

Ingredients:

- 1 tablespoon of butter
- ¼ cup of white sugar
- ¼ cup of balsamic vinegar

- 2 tablespoons of olive oil
- 2 large red onions, should be thinly sliced
- 1 cup of dry red wine
- 1 pinch of salt to taste

Direction:

1. Heat butter together with olive oil in a large skillet and place on medium heat. Cook and stir sugar and onions in hot oil until the onions start to caramelize in about 15 minutes. Then stir balsamic vinegar and red wine into the onion mixture and let it boil. Reduce the heat to medium-low and simmer until all the liquid is evaporated in about 15-20 minutes—finally, season with salt.

Nutrition: 111.5 calories Carbohydrates 11.7 grams 4% Protein 0.5 grams 1% Fat 4.9 grams 8 Cholesterol 3.8 mg 1% Sodium 14.9 mg 1%.

Jamaican Fried Dumplings

Preparation Time: 10 Minutes

Cooking Time: 20 Minutes

Servings: 6

Ingredients:

- 2 teaspoons of baking powder
- ½ cup of butter
- 1 cup of vegetable oil for frying
- 4 cups of all-purpose flour
- 1 ½ teaspoons of salt
- ½ cup of cold water

Direction:

1. Get a large bowl and stir together the baking powder, flour, and salt. Rub in the butter, and its sizes are not to be larger than peas. Mix in 1 tablespoon of water until the mixture is wet enough to form a ball. Note that the dough should be firm all through. Then, knead briefly.

2. Pour the oil you want to use in a heavy skillet and apply medium heat until it gets hot. Then break off the dough pieces and form them to a patty shape — just like a flat biscuit. Then place as many of the dumplings as the pan can take, so they do not become overcrowded. Fry on each of the sides until they become golden brown using about 3 minutes for each side. Then remove from the pan and drain on paper towels before you serve.

Nutrition: 472.2 calories Carbohydrates 64 grams 21% Protein 8.8 grams 18% Fat 19.8 grams 31% Cholesterol 40.7 mg 14% Sodium 855.1 mg 34%

Mango Snacks

Preparation Time: 10 Minutes

Cooking Time: 3 Hours

Servings: 4

Ingredients: 2 ripe mangoes

Direction:

1. Preheat the oven to 185°F or as low as your oven could go. Put a Silpat silicone mat on the baking sheet

2. Wash the 2 mangoes and use a peeler in removing their skin

3. Cut the mangoes into thin slices and place them on the Silpat

4. Put the mangoes in the oven and bake for 2 or 3 hours, and you should flip them to the other side every 30 minutes until they become dry. It is important to avoid cooking them for too long to not end up with mango chips!

5. Store any leftovers in airtight containers. Since they are preservative-free, you can enjoy them for a few days.

Nutrition: 67 calories Carbohydrates 17.5 grams 6% Protein 0.5 grams Fat 0.5 grams 1% Sodium 2 mg

Baked Banana Fritters

Preparation Time: 10 Minutes

Cooking Time: 20 Minutes

Servings: 4

Ingredients:

- 2 tablespoons of dry shredded coconuts
- ¼ teaspoon of ground cinnamon
- 2 medium (7" to 7-7/8" long) bananas, to be cut into bite-size pieces
- 1/3 cup of dry breadcrumbs
- 1 teaspoon of white sugar
- 1 egg white

Direction:

1. Preheat the oven to 350°F (175°C). Line the baking sheet with parchment paper.
2. Combine coconut, breadcrumbs, cinnamon, and sugar in a bowl. Beat egg white in a small bowl until it becomes frothy. Dip each banana piece in egg white and press into the bread crumb mixture. Then put the breaded bananas on the already prepared baking sheet, do not stack.
3. Bake in the already preheated oven until it turns golden brown in about 10 minutes.

Nutrition: 111.8 calories Carbohydrates 20.8 grams 7% Protein 3 grams 6% Fat 2.6 grams 4% Sodium 81.4 mg 34%

Air Fryer Avocado Fries

Preparation Time: 10 Minutes

Cooking Time: 20 Minutes

Servings: 2

Ingredients:

- ¼ cup of all-purpose flour
- 1/4 teaspoon of salt
- 1 teaspoon of water
- ½ cup of panko breadcrumbs
- ½ teaspoon of ground black pepper
- 1 egg
- 1 ripe avocado, should be halved, seeded, and peeled before cutting into 8 slices
- 1 serving cooking spray

Direction:

1. Preheat air fryer to about 400°F (200°C)
2. Mix the pepper, flour, and salt in a shallow bowl. Get another shallow bowl and beat water and egg together in it. Then put panko in a third shallow bowl.
3. Dredge an avocado slice through the flour, but you should shake off any excess. Dip into the egg and let the excess fall off. Finally, press slice into the panko so that both sides are well covered. Set on a plate and repeat this process with the remaining slices
4. Spray avocado slices generously with cooking spray and arrange in the air fryer bowl, should be sprayed side-down. Spray the top part of the avocado slices also.
5. Cook in the already preheated air fryer for about 4 minutes. Turn the avocado slices over and cook until they become golden in about 3 minutes.

Nutrition: 319 calories Carbohydrates 39.8 grams 13% Protein 9.3 grams 19% Fat 18 grams 28% Cholesterol 81.8 mg 27% Sodium 452.9 mg 19%

Hunter's Beet Chips

Preparation Time: 15 Minutes

Cooking Time: 45 Minutes

Servings: 4

Ingredients:

- 5 large beets, peeled thinly and sliced
- 1 pinch of salt and ground black pepper to taste
- 1 serving cooking spray
- 1 tablespoon of olive oil or as required

Direction:

1. Preheat your oven to 400°F (200°C). Spray the baking sheet with a cooking spray
2. Spread the beets out in a single layer and on the already prepared baking sheet. Brush beets on their 2 sides with olive oil and season with pepper and salt.
3. Then bake in the already preheated oven for 15 minutes. Turn the beets and keep cooking until it becomes crisp in about 15-20 minutes. Transfer the chips to a wire rack for it to cool.

Nutrition: 163.7 calories Carbohydrates 29.6 grams 10% Protein 5 grams 10% Fat 4 grams 6% Cholesterol 81.8 mg 27% Sodium 241.9 mg 10%

Artichokes in a Garlic together with Olive Oil Sauce

Preparation Time: 10 Minutes

Cooking Time: 25 Minutes

Servings: 2

Ingredients:

- 2 ½ tablespoons of extra virgin olive oil

- 2 cloves of garlic
- 1 (8 ounces) can artichoke hearts, to be drained and quartered
- 4 ounces of small uncooked seashell pasta
- 3 tablespoons of butter
- 1 sprig of fresh basil, to be chopped.

Direction:

1. Get a pot of lightly salted water to boil. Add seashell pasta, cook for 8 to 10 minutes until it is al dente, and drain.
2. Put the butter and olive oil in a skillet and met with medium heat. Mix in the basil, garlic, and artichoke hearts and cook for like 5 minutes until they become heated all through. Toss with the cooked pasta and serve.

Nutrition: 590.9 calories Carbohydrates 56.3 grams 18% Protein 12.6 grams 25% Fat 35.5 grams 55% Cholesterol 45.8 mg 15% Sodium 804.7 mg 32%

Louisiana Crab Dip

Preparation Time: 15 Minutes

Cooking Time: 50 Minutes

Servings: 8

Ingredients:

- 2 tablespoons unsalted butter
- 3 garlic cloves, minced
- ½ cup mayonnaise
- 1 pound (16 ounces) whipped or room temperature cream cheese
- 2 teaspoons Worcestershire sauce
- 3 teaspoons hot sauce
- 3 teaspoons freshly squeezed lemon juice
- 2 teaspoons Creole seasoning
- ¾ cup Parmesan cheese
- 1-pound lump crab meat

Directions:

1. Select SEAR/SAUTÉ and set to MED. Select START/STOP to begin. Let preheat for 3 minutes.
2. Add the butter and garlic and sauté for 2 minutes.
3. Add the mayonnaise, cream cheese, Worcestershire sauce, hot sauce, lemon juice, Creole seasoning, and Parmesan cheese. Stir well.
4. Add the crab meat and lightly fold to incorporate. Close crisping lid.
5. Select BAKE/ROAST, set the temperature to 350°F, and set the time to 40 minutes. Select START/STOP to begin
6. When cooking is complete, open the lid. Let cool for 10 minutes before serving.

Nutrition: Calories: 391; Total Fat: 39g; Saturated Fat: 18g; Cholesterol: 114mg; Sodium: 976mg; Carbohydrates: 4g; Fiber: 0g; Protein: 16g

Three-Layer Taco Dip

Preparation Time: 10 Minutes

Cooking Time: 15 Minutes

Servings: 6

Ingredients:

- 2 (15.5-ounce) cans pinto beans, rinsed and drained
- 1 white onion, chopped
- 8 garlic cloves, chopped
- 1 (14.5-ounce) can diced tomatoes
- 1 serrano chile, seeded and chopped
- 1 teaspoon kosher salt
- 2 teaspoons ground cumin
- 2 teaspoons chili powder
- 2 cups shredded Mexican blend cheese
- 1 cup shredded iceberg lettuce

Directions:

1. Place the beans, onions, garlic, tomatoes, chile, salt, cumin, and chili powder in the pot. Assemble the pressure lid, making sure the pressure release valve is in the SEAL position.
2. Select PRESSURE and set it to HI. Set time to 5 minutes. Select START/STOP to begin.
3. When pressure cooking is complete, quick release the pressure by moving the pressure release valve to the VENT position. Carefully remove lid when the unit has finished releasing pressure.
4. Using a silicone spatula, stir the mixture in the pot. Sprinkle shredded cheese across the top of the bean mixture. Close crisping lid.
5. Select BROIL and set the time to 10 minutes. Select STOP/START to begin.
6. When cooking is complete, open the lid. Let cool for 5 minutes, then add the shredded lettuce. Serve immediately.

Nutrition: Calories: 327; Total Fat: 14g; Saturated Fat: 9g; Cholesterol: 46mg; Sodium: 612mg; Carbohydrates: 33g; Fiber: 10g; Protein: 19g

Mexican Street Corn Queso Dip

Preparation Time: 10 Minutes

Cooking Time: 20 Minutes

Servings: 8

Ingredients:

- 1 (8-ounce) package cream cheese, quartered
- 6 ounces cotija cheese, crumbled, 2 ounces reserved for topping
- 1 (10-ounce) can fire-roasted tomatoes with chiles
- ½ cup mayonnaise
- Zest of 2 limes
- Juice of 2 limes
- 2 (8-ounce) packages shredded Mexican cheese blend, divided

- 1 garlic clove, grated
- 1 (14.75-ounce) can cream corn
- 1 cup of frozen corn
- Kosher salt
- Freshly ground black pepper

Directions:

1. Pour the cream cheese, 4 ounces of cotija cheese, tomatoes with chiles, mayonnaise, lime zest, and juice, one 8-ounce package Mexican cheese blend, garlic, cream corn, and frozen corn in the pot. Season with salt and pepper and stir. Close crisping lid.
2. Select BAKE/ROAST, set the temperature to 375°F, and set the time to 20 minutes. Select START/STOP to begin.
3. After 10 minutes, open the lid and sprinkle the dip with the remaining 2 ounces of cotija cheese and remaining 8-ounce package of Mexican blend cheese. Close the crisping lid and continue cooking.
4. When cooking is complete, the cheese will be melted and the dip hot and bubbling at the edges. Open the lid and let the dip cool for 5 to 10 minutes before serving. Serve topped with chopped cilantro, hot sauce, and chili powder, if desired.

Nutrition: Calories: 538; Total Fat: 45g; Saturated Fat: 22g; Cholesterol: 109mg; Sodium: 807mg; Carbohydrates: 18g; Fiber: 2g; Protein: 20g

Mexican Street Corn

Preparation Time: 10 Minutes

Cooking Time: 14 Minutes

Servings: 3

Ingredients:

- 3 ears corn, husked, rinsed and dried
- Olive oil spray

- ¼ cup sour cream
- ¼ cup mayonnaise
- ¼ cup crumbled cotija cheese, plus more for garnish
- 1 teaspoon freshly squeezed lime juice
- ½ teaspoon garlic powder
- ¼ teaspoon chili powder, plus more as needed
- Fresh cilantro leaves, for garnish
- ½ teaspoon salt
- ½ teaspoon freshly ground black pepper

Directions:

1. Select AIR CRISP, set the temperature to 400°F, and set the time to 5 minutes to preheat. Select START/STOP to begin.
2. Lightly mist the corn with olive oil and place the corn in the Cook & Crisp Basket. Close the crisping lid.
3. Select AIR CRISP, set the temperature to 400°F, and set the time to 12 minutes. Select START/STOP to begin. After 7 minutes, flip the corn. Close the crisping lid and cook for 5 minutes more.
4. While the corn cooks, in a small bowl, stir together the sour cream, mayonnaise, cotija cheese, lime juice, garlic powder, and chili powder until blended.
5. When cooking is complete, carefully remove the corn and brush or spoon the sauce onto it. Sprinkle with cilantro, cotija cheese, and more chili powder.
6. If desired, return the corn to the basket. Close the crisping lid. Select BROIL and set the time for 2 minutes. Select START/STOP to begin.
7. Serve hot, seasoned with salt and pepper, as needed.

Nutrition: Calories: 280; Total Fat: 15g; Saturated Fat: 6g; Cholesterol: 25mg; Sodium: 701mg; Carbohydrates: 35g; Fiber: 4g; Protein: 7g

Zucchini Chips

Preparation Time: 15 Minutes

Cooking Time: 13 Minutes

Servings: 6

Ingredients:

- 1 large egg, beaten
- ¾ cup panko bread crumbs
- 1 teaspoon Old Bay seasoning
- 1 teaspoon garlic salt
- ½ teaspoon kosher salt
- 2 large zucchinis, ends trimmed cut into ¼- to ½-inch rounds (the thinner the crispier)
- Olive oil spray

Directions:

1. Place the Cook & Crisp Basket into the unit. Select AIR CRISP, set the temperature to 350°F, and set the time to 5 minutes to preheat. Select START/STOP to begin.
2. Place the beaten egg in a shallow bowl. In another shallow bowl, stir together the panko, Old Bay seasoning, garlic salt, and kosher salt.
3. One at a time, dip the zucchini rounds into the egg and the panko mixture, coating all sides. Working in batches as needed, place the coated zucchini chips in the Cook & Crisp Basket in a single layer so they do not overlap. Coat the pieces with cooking spray and place them into the preheated Cook & Crisp Basket.
4. Select AIR CRISP, set the temperature to 350°F, and set the time to 13 minutes. Select START/STOP to begin. After 10 minutes, flip the zucchini. Close the crisping lid and cook for 3 minutes more, or longer for crispier results.
5. Remove and repeat with the second batch.

Nutrition: Calories: 59; Total Fat: 2g; Saturated Fat: 0g; Cholesterol: 31mg; Sodium: 374mg; Carbohydrates: 9g; Fiber: 2g; Protein: 3g

Nutrition: Calories: 171; Total Fat: 11g; Saturated Fat: 1g; Cholesterol: 0mg; Sodium: 7mg; Carbohydrates: 18g; Fiber: 3g; Protein: 2g

Hand-Cut French Fries

Preparation Time: 15 Minutes

Cooking Time: 25 Minutes

Servings: 4

Ingredients:

- 1-pound Russet or Idaho potatoes, cut in 2-inch strips
- 3 tablespoons canola oil

Directions:

1. Place potatoes in a large bowl and cover with cold water. Let soak for 30 minutes. Drain well, then pat with a paper towel until very dry.
2. Place Cook & Crisp Basket in the pot. Close crisping lid. Select AIR CRISP, set temperature to 390°F, and set time to 5 minutes. Select START/STOP to begin preheating.
3. In a large bowl, toss the potatoes with the oil.
4. Once the unit is preheated, open the lid and add the potatoes to the basket. Close lid.
5. Select AIR CRISP, set the temperature to 390°F, and set the time to 25 minutes. Select START/STOP to begin.
6. After 10 minutes, open the lid, then lift the basket and shake fries or toss them with silicone-tipped tongs. Lower basket back into the pot and close lid to continue cooking.
7. After 10 minutes, check for desired crispness. Continue cooking up to 5 minutes more, if necessary.
8. When cooking is complete, serve immediately with your favorite dipping sauce.

Sweet Potato and Beetroot Chips

Preparation Time: 15 Minutes

Cooking Time: 8 Hours

Servings: 1 Cup

Ingredients:

- ½ small beet, peeled and cut into 1/8-inch slices
- ½ small sweet potato, peeled and cut into 1/8-inch slices
- ½ tablespoon extra-virgin olive oil
- ½ teaspoon sea salt

Directions:

1. In a large bowl, toss the beet slices with half the olive oil until evenly coated. Repeat, in a separate bowl, with the sweet potato slices and the rest of the olive oil (if you don't mind pink sweet potatoes, you can toss them together in one bowl). Season with salt.
2. Arrange the beet slices flat in a single layer in the bottom of the pot. Arrange the sweet potato slices flat in a single layer on the Reversible Rack in the lower position. Place rack in pot and close crisping lid.
3. Select DEHYDRATE, set the temperature to 135°F, and set the time to 8 hours. Select START/STOP to begin.
4. When dehydrating is complete, remove the rack from the pot. Transfer the beet and sweet potato chips to an airtight container.

Nutrition: Calories: 221; Total Fat: 7g; Saturated Fat: 1g; Cholesterol: 0mg; Sodium: 1057mg; Carbohydrates: 36g; Fiber: 6g; Protein: 4g

Loaded Potato Skins

Preparation Time: 5 Minutes

Cooking Time: 45 Minutes

Servings: 4

Ingredients:

- 2 large Russet potatoes, cleaned
- 1 tablespoon extra-virgin olive oil
- Kosher salt
- Freshly ground black pepper
- ¾ cup shredded sharp Cheddar cheese
- 3 tablespoons unsalted butter
- ¼ cup milk
- ¼ cup sour cream, plus more for serving
- 1 bunch chives, sliced
- 4 slices of ham, cubed

Directions:

1. Using a fork, poke holes in each potato. Rub each potato with olive oil and season the skin with salt and pepper. Place the potatoes on the Reversible Rack in the lower position and place them in the pot. Close the crisping lid.
2. Select AIR CRISP, set the temperature to 390°F, and set the time to 35 minutes. Select START/STOP to begin.
3. When cooking is complete, open the lid and use tongs to transfer the potatoes to a cutting board.
4. Cut the potatoes in half lengthwise. Using a spoon, scoop out the flesh into a large bowl, leaving about ¼ inch of flesh on the skins. Set aside.
5. Sprinkle the hollowed-out potato skins with ¼ cup of cheese and place them back in the pot on the rack. Close crisping lid.
6. Select BROIL and set the time to 5 minutes. Select START/STOP to begin.
7. Add the butter, milk, and sour cream to the bowl with the flesh. Season with salt and pepper and mash together.

Use a spatula to fold in ¼ cup of cheese, one-quarter of the chives, and ham into the potato mixture.
8. When cooking is complete, open the lid. Using tongs, carefully transfer the potato skins to the cutting board. Evenly distribute the mashed potato mixture into each potato skin and top with the remaining ¼ cup of cheese. Return the loaded potato skins to the rack. Close crisping lid.
9. Select BROIL and set the time to 5 minutes. Select START/STOP to begin.
10. When cooking is complete, open the lid. Carefully remove the potatoes. Cut them in half and garnish with the remaining chives. Serve with additional sour cream, if desired.

Nutrition: Calories: 402; Total Fat: 24g; Saturated Fat: 14g; Cholesterol: 68mg; Sodium: 561mg; Carbohydrates: 32g; Fiber: 5g; Protein: 14g

Sponge Cake

Preparation time: 10 minutes

Cooking time: 20 minutes

Servings: 12

Ingredients:

- 3 cups flour
- 3 teaspoons baking powder
- ½ cup cornstarch
- 1 teaspoon baking soda
- 1 cup olive oil
- 1 and ½ cup milk
- 1 and 2/3 cup sugar
- 2 cups water
- ¼ cup lemon juice
- 2 teaspoons vanilla extract

Directions:

1. Inside a bowl, mix flour with baking powder, baking soda, cornstarch, and sugar and whisk well.

2. In another bowl, mix oil with milk, water, vanilla, and lemon juice and whisk.
3. Combine the two mixtures, stir, pour in a greased baking dish that fits your air fryer, introduce in the fryer, and cook at 350 0 F for 20 minutes.
4. Leave the cake to cool down, cut, and serve.
5. Enjoy!

Nutrition: Calories 246, Fat 3, Fiber 1, Carbs 6, Protein 2

Ricotta and Lemon Cake

Preparation time: 10 minutes

Cooking time: 1 hour and 10 minutes

Servings: 4

Ingredients:

- 8 eggs, whisked
- 3 pounds ricotta cheese
- ½ pound sugar
- Zest from 1 lemon, grated
- Zest from 1 orange, grated
- Butter for the pan

Directions:

1. In a bowl, mix eggs with sugar, cheese, lemon, and orange zest and stir very well.
2. Grease a baking pan that fits your air fryer with some batter, spread ricotta mixture, introduce in the fryer at 390 0 F and bake for 30 minutes.
3. Reduce heat at 380 0 F and bake for 40 more minutes.
4. Take out of the oven, leave the cake to cool down, and serve!
5. Enjoy!

Nutrition: Calories 110, Fat 3, Fiber 2, Carbs 3, Protein 4

Tangerine Cake

Preparation time: 10 minutes

Cooking time: 20 minutes

Servings: 8

Ingredients:

- ¾ cup sugar
- 2 cups flour
- ¼ cup olive oil
- ½ cup milk
- 1 teaspoon cider vinegar
- ½ teaspoon vanilla extract
- Juice and zest from 2 lemons
- Juice and zest from 1 tangerine
- Tangerine segments, for serving

Directions:

1. In a bowl, mix flour with sugar and stir.
2. In another bowl, mix oil with milk, vinegar, vanilla extract, lemon juice, and zest and tangerine zest and whisk very well.
3. Add flour, stir well, pour this into a cake pan that fits your air fryer, introduce in the fryer, and cook at 360 0 F for 20 minutes.
4. Serve right away with tangerine segments on top.
5. Enjoy!

Nutrition: Calories 180, Fat 2, Fiber 1, Carbs 4, Protein 4

Berries Mix

Preparation time: 5 minutes

Cooking time: 6 minutes

Servings: 4

Ingredients:

- 2 tablespoons lemon juice
- 1 and ½ tablespoons maple syrup
- 1 and ½ tablespoons champagne vinegar
- 1 tablespoon olive oil
- 1-pound strawberries halved
- 1 and ½ cups blueberries
- ¼ cup basil leaves, torn

Directions:

1. In a pan that sizes your air fryer, mix lemon juice with maple syrup and vinegar, bring to a boil over medium-high heat, add oil, blueberries, and strawberries, stir, introduce in your air fryer and cook at 310 0 F for 6 minutes.
2. Sprinkle basil on top and serve!
3. Enjoy!

Nutrition: Calories 163, Fat 4, Fiber 4, Carbs 10, Protein 2.1

Passion Fruit Pudding

Preparation time: 10 minutes

Cooking time: 40 minutes

Servings: 6

Ingredients:

- 1 cup Paleo passion fruit curd
- 4 passion fruits, pulp, and seeds
- 3 and ½ ounces maple syrup
- 3 eggs
- 2 ounces ghee, melted
- 3 and ½ ounces of almond milk
- ½ cup almond flour
- ½ teaspoon baking powder

Directions:

1. In a bowl, mix half of the fruit curd with passion fruit seeds and pulp, stir and divide into 6 heatproof ramekins.
2. In a bowl, whisk eggs with maple syrup, ghee, the rest of the curd, baking powder, milk, and flour, and stir well.

3. Divide this into the ramekins as well, introduce in the fryer and cook at 200 0 F for 40 minutes.
4. Leave puddings to cool down and serve!
5. Enjoy!

Nutrition: Calories 430, Fat 22, Fiber 3, Carbs 7, Protein 8

Air Fried Apples

Preparation time: 10 minutes

Cooking time: 17 minutes

Servings: 4

Ingredients:

- 4 big apples, cored
- A handful of raisins
- 1 tablespoon cinnamon, ground
- Raw honey to the taste

Directions:

1. Fill each apple with raisins, sprinkle cinnamon, drizzle honey, put them in your air fryer, and cook at 367 0 F for 17 minutes.
2. Leave them to cool down and serve.
3. Enjoy!

Nutrition: Calories 220, Fat 3, Fiber 4, Carbs 6, Protein 10

Pumpkin Cookies

Preparation time: 10 minutes

Cooking time: 15 minutes

Servings: 24

Ingredients:

- 2 and ½ cups flour
- ½ teaspoon baking soda

- 1 tablespoon flax seed, ground
- 3 tablespoons water
- ½ cup pumpkin flesh, mashed
- ¼ cup honey
- 2 tablespoons butter
- 1 teaspoon vanilla extract
- ½ cup dark chocolate chips

Directions:

1. In a bowl, mix flaxseed with water, stir and leave aside for a few minutes.
2. Mix flour with salt and baking soda in another bowl.
3. In a third bowl, mix honey with pumpkin puree, butter, vanilla extract, and flaxseed.
4. Combine flour with honey mix and chocolate chips and stir.
5. Scoop 1 tablespoon of cookie dough on a lined baking sheet that fits your air fryer, repeat with the rest of the dough, introduce them in your air fryer and cook at 350 0 F for 15 minutes.
6. Leave cookies to cool down and serve.
7. Enjoy it!

Nutrition: Calories 140, Fat 2, Fiber 2, Carbs 7, Protein 10

Tasty Orange Cookies

Preparation time: 10 minutes

Cooking time: 12 minutes

Servings: 8

Ingredients:

- 2 cups flour
- 1 teaspoon baking powder
- ½ cup butter, soft
- ¾ cup sugar
- 1 egg, whisked
- 1 teaspoon vanilla extract
- 1 tablespoon orange zest, grated
- For the filling:
- 4 ounces cream cheese, soft
- ½ cup butter
- 2 cups powdered sugar

Directions:

1. In a bowl, mix cream cheese with ½ cup butter and 2 cups powdered sugar, stir well using your mixer and leave aside for now.
2. In another bowl, mix flour with baking powder.
3. In a third bowl, mix ½ cup butter with ¾ cup sugar, egg, vanilla extract, and orange zest and whisk well.
4. Combine flour with the orange mix, stir well and scoop 1 tablespoon of the mix on a lined baking sheet that fits your air fryer.
5. Repeat with the rest of the orange batter, introduce in the fryer, and cook at 340 0 F for 12 minutes.
6. Leave cookies to cool down, spread cream filling on half of the top with the other cookies, and serve.
7. Enjoy!

Nutrition: Calories 124, Fat 5, Fiber 6, Carbs 8, Protein 4

Chicken

Chicken Alfredo Apples

Preparation Time: 5-10 Minutes

Cooking Time: 20 Minutes

Servings: 4

Ingredients:

- 1 large apple, wedged
- 1 tablespoon lemon juice
- 4 chicken breasts, halved
- 4 teaspoons chicken seasoning
- 4 slices provolone cheese
- 1/4 cup blue cheese, crumbled
- 1/2 cup Alfredo sauce

Directions:

1. Season the chicken in a bowl with chicken seasoning. In another bowl, toss the apple with lemon juice.

2. Take Ninja Grill, arrange it over your kitchen platform, and open the top lid.
3. Arrange the grill grate and close the top lid.
4. Press "GRILL" and select the "MED" grill function. Adjust the timer to 16 minutes and then press "START /STOP." The Ninja will start pre-heating.
5. Ninja is preheated and ready to cook when it starts to beep. After you hear a beep, open the top lid.
6. Arrange the chicken over the grill grate.
7. Close the top lid and cook for 8 minutes. Now open the top lid, flip the chicken.
8. Close the top lid and cook for 8 more minutes.
9. Then, grill the apple in the same manner for 2 minutes per side.
10. Serve the chicken with the apple, blue cheese, and Alfredo sauce.

Nutrition: Calories: 247 Fat: 19g Saturated Fat: 3g Trans Fat: 0g Carbohydrates: 29.5g Fiber: 2g Sodium: 853mg Protein: 14.5g

Baked Soy Chicken

Preparation Time: 5-10 Minutes

Cooking Time: 25 Minutes

Servings: 5-6

Ingredients:

- 1 /2 cup soy sauce
- 1 /4 cup apple cider vinegar
- 1 clove garlic, minced
- 1 tablespoon cornstarch
- 1 tablespoon cold water
- 1 /2 cup white sugar
- 1 /4 teaspoon ground black pepper
- 1 /2 teaspoon ground ginger
- 12 skinless chicken thighs

Directions:

1. In a mixing bowl, add the cornstarch, water, white sugar, soy sauce, apple cider vinegar, garlic, ginger, and black pepper. Combine the ingredients to mix well with each other.
2. Season the chicken with salt and ground black pepper.
3. Take a multi-purpose pan and lightly grease it with some cooking oil. In the pan, add the chicken and add the soy mixture on top.
4. Take Ninja Foodi Grill, arrange it over your kitchen platform, and open the top lid.
5. Press "BAKE" and adjust the temperature to 350°F. Adjust the timer to 25 minutes and then press "START /STOP." Ninja Foodi will start preheating.
6. Ninja Foodi is preheated and ready to cook when it starts to beep. After you hear a beep, open the top lid.
7. Arrange the pan directly inside the pot.

8. Close the top lid and allow it to cook until the timer reads zero.
9. Serve warm.

Nutrition: Calories: 573 Fat: 19g Saturated Fat: 5g Trans Fat: 0g Carbohydrates: 23.5g Fiber: 1g Sodium: 624mg Protein: 48.5g

Salsa Coconut Chicken

Preparation Time: 5-10 Minutes

Cooking Time: 12 Minutes

Servings: 4

Ingredients:

- ½ cup of coconut milk
- ¼ cup chicken broth
- Black pepper (ground) and salt to taste
- 1 large yellow onion, chopped
- 1 cup salsa Verde
- 4 chicken breasts, cut into 1-inch cubes

Directions:

1. Take Ninja Foodi multi-cooker, arrange it over a cooking platform, and open the top lid.
2. In the pot, add all the ingredients and combine well.
3. Seal the multi-cooker by locking it with the pressure lid; ensure to keep the pressure release valve locked /sealed.
4. Select the "PRESSURE" mode and select the "HI" pressure level. Then, set the timer to 12 minutes and press "STOP /START"; it will start the cooking process by building up inside pressure.
5. When the timer goes off, naturally release inside pressure for about 8-10 minutes. Then, quick-release pressure by adjusting the pressure valve to the VENT.
6. Serve warm and enjoy!

Nutrition: Calories: 548 Fat: 29g Saturated Fat: 5g Trans Fat: 0g Carbohydrates: 7g Fiber: 2.5g Sodium: 847mg Protein: 61g

Chicken Coconut Curry

Preparation Time: 5-10 Minutes

Cooking Time: 12 Minutes

Servings: 4

Ingredients:

- 1 yellow bell pepper, deseeded and thinly sliced
- 1 red bell pepper, deseeded and thinly sliced
- 4 chicken thighs
- Black pepper (ground) and salt to taste
- 1 tablespoon olive oil
- 1 garlic clove, minced
- 1 ½ cups cauliflower rice
- 2 tablespoons red curry paste
- 1 teaspoon ginger paste
- ¼ cup coconut of milk
- ½ cup chicken broth
- 2 tablespoons chopped cilantro to garnish
- 1 lime, cut into wedges to garnish

Directions:

1. Season, the chicken with salt and black pepper.
2. Take Ninja Foodi multi-cooker, arrange it over a cooking platform, and open the top lid.
3. In the pot, add the oil; Select "SEAR /SAUTÉ" mode and select "MD: HI" pressure level. Press "STOP /START." After about 4-5 minutes, the oil will start simmering.
4. Add the meat and stir cook for about 5-6 minutes to brown evenly. Set aside the chicken.
5. Add the bell peppers and cook (while stirring) until it becomes softened. Add

the curry paste, ginger, and garlic; stir-cook until fragrant, 1 minute.
6. Add the cauliflower rice, chicken broth, coconut milk; stir the mixture. Add the chicken and combine well.
7. Seal the multi-cooker by locking it with the pressure lid; ensure to keep the pressure release valve locked /sealed.
8. Select "PRESSURE" mode and select the "HI" pressure level. Then, set the timer to 4 minutes and press "STOP /START"; it will start the cooking process by building up inside pressure.
9. When the timer goes off, quick release pressure by adjusting the pressure valve to the VENT. After pressure gets released, open the pressure lid. Serve warm with the cilantro, lime wedges.

Nutrition: Calories: 523 Fat: 28.5g Saturated Fat: 5g Trans Fat: 0g Carbohydrates: 11g Fiber: 2g Sodium: 942mg Protein: 37.5g

Chicken Paillards with Fresh Tomato Sauce

Preparation Time: 5 minutes

Cooking Time: 4 minutes

Serving: 4

Ingredients:

- 2 whole skinless, boneless chicken breasts (each 12 to 16 ounces, or 4 half breasts (each half 6 to 8 ounces
- 1 clove garlic, minced
- 3 fresh basil leaves, minced, plus 4 basil sprigs for garnish
- Coarse salt (kosher or sea and freshly ground black pepper
- 2 tablespoons extra-virgin olive oil

TOMATO SAUCE

- 1 clove garlic, minced
- ½ teaspoon salt, or more to taste

- 1 large ripe red tomato (6 to 8 ounces, seeded (see Tips and cut into ¼-inch dice
- 12 niçoise olives, or 6 black olives, pitted and cut into ¼-inch dice
- 8 fresh basil leaves, thinly slivered
- ¼ cup extra-virgin olive oil
- 1 tablespoon red wine vinegar, or more to taste
- Freshly ground black pepper

Directions:

1. If using whole chicken breasts, divide them in half. Trim any sinews or excess fat off the chicken breasts and discard. Remove the tenders from the breasts and set them aside. Rinse the breasts under cold running water, then drain. Place a breast half between 2 pieces of plastic wrap and gently pound it to a thickness of between ¼ and 1 /8 inch using a meat pounder, the side of a heavy cleaver, a rolling pin, or the bottom of a heavy saucepan. Repeat with the remaining breast halves.
2. Place the garlic and minced basil, ½ teaspoon of salt, and ½ teaspoon of pepper in a bowl and mash to a paste with the back of a spoon. Stir in the olive oil. Brush each paillard on both sides with the garlic and basil mixture and season lightly with salt and pepper.
3. Insert the Grill Grate and close the hood. Select GRILL, set the temperature to HIGH, and set the time to 4 minutes. Select START /STOP to begin preheating.

Nutrition: Calories 299 Fat 20 g Protein 52 g

BBQ Chicken Broccoli

Preparation Time: 5-10 Minutes

Cooking Time: 15 Minutes

Servings: 4

Ingredients:

- 4 chicken tenders
- ¼ cup sugar-free barbecue sauce
- 2 lemons, juiced
- 1 head broccoli, cut into florets
- ½ tablespoon coconut aminos
- 2 tablespoons melted butter
- Black pepper (ground) and salt to taste
- 1 tablespoon sesame seeds to garnish
- 2 tablespoons freshly chopped scallions to garnish

Directions:

1. In a medium bowl, combine the broccoli with half portion butter, salt, and black pepper. Brush the chicken with the remaining butter. In a mixing bowl, mix the barbecue sauce, lemon juice, and coconut aminos.
2. Take Ninja Foodi multi-cooker, arrange it over a cooking platform, and open the top lid. In the pot, arrange a reversible rack and place the Crisping Basket over the rack. In the basket, add the chicken and broccoli mixture around the meat.
3. Seal the multi-cooker by locking it with the crisping lid; ensure to keep the pressure release valve locked /sealed.
4. Select the "AIR CRISP" mode and adjust the 375°F temperature level. Then, set the timer to 10 minutes and press "STOP /START"; it will start the cooking process by building up inside pressure.
5. When the timer goes off, quick release pressure by adjusting the pressure valve to the VENT.
6. After pressure gets released, open the pressure lid. Brush the chicken with a BBQ mixture.
7. Seal the multi-cooker by locking it with the crisping lid; ensure to keep the pressure release valve locked /sealed.
8. Select "BROIL" mode and select the "HI" pressure level. Then, set the timer to 5 minutes and press "STOP /START"; it will start the cooking process by building up inside pressure.

9. When the timer goes off, quick release pressure by adjusting the pressure valve to the VENT. After pressure gets released, open the pressure lid. Serve warm and enjoy!

Nutrition: Calories: 743 Fat: 24.5g Saturated Fat: 4g Trans Fat: 0g Carbohydrates: 8.5g Fiber: 3 Sodium: 952mg Protein: 52g

Orange Curried Chicken Stir-Fry

Preparation Time: 10 minutes

Cooking Time: 18 minutes

Serving: 4

Ingredients:

- ¾ pound boneless, skinless chicken thighs, cut into 1-inch pieces
- 1 yellow bell pepper, cut into 1½-inch pieces
- 1 small red onion, sliced
- Olive oil for misting
- ¼ cup chicken stock
- 2 tablespoons honey
- ¼ cup orange juice
- 1 tablespoon cornstarch
- 2 to 3 teaspoons curry powder

Directions:

1. Insert the Crisper Basket, and close the hood. Select AIR CRISP, set the temperature to 165°F, and set the time to 15 minutes. Select START /STOP to begin preheating.
2. Put the chicken thighs, pepper, and red onion in the air fryer basket and mist with olive oil.

Nutrition: Calories 299 Fat 20 g Protein 52 g

Balsamic-Rosemary Chicken Breasts

Preparation Time: 5 minutes

Cooking Time: 6 minutes

Serving: 4

Ingredients:

- ½ cup balsamic vinegar
- 2 tablespoons olive oil
- 2 rosemary sprigs, coarsely chopped
- 2 pounds boneless, skinless chicken breasts, pounded to the ½-inch thickness

Directions:

1. Combine the balsamic vinegar, olive oil, and rosemary in a shallow baking dish. Add the chicken breasts and turn to coat. Cover with plastic wrap and refrigerate for at least 30 minutes or overnight.
2. Insert the Grill Grate and close the hood. Select GRILL, set the temperature to HIGH, and set the time to 6 minutes. Select START /STOP to begin preheating.
3. When the unit beeps to signify it has preheated, place the s chicken breasts on the Grill Grate. Close the hood and cook for 6 minutes until they have taken on grill marks and are cooked through.

Nutrition: Calories 299 Fat 20 g Protein 52 g

Chicken Fajitas

Preparation Time: 10 minutes

Cooking Time: 15 minutes

Serving: 4

Ingredients:

- 4 boneless, skinless chicken breasts, sliced
- 1 small red onion, sliced
- 2 red bell peppers, sliced
- ½ cup spicy ranch salad dressing, divided
- ½ teaspoon dried oregano
- 8 corn tortillas
- 2 cups torn butter lettuce
- avocados, peeled and chopped

Directions:

1. Insert the Crisper Basket, and close the hood. Select AIR CRISP, set the temperature to 165°F, and set the time to 15 minutes. Select START /STOP to begin preheating.
2. Place the chicken, onion, and pepper in the air fryer basket. Drizzle with 1 tablespoon of the salad dressing and add the oregano. Toss to combine.

Nutrition: Calories 783 Fat 38 g Protein 72 g Fiber 12 g

Super Barbeque Chicken

Preparation Time: 5-10 Minutes

Cooking Time: 12 Minutes

Servings: 3-4

Ingredients:

- 6 chicken drumsticks
- 2 teaspoon BBQ seasoning
- 1 pinch teaspoon salt
- ½ cup ketchup
- 1 tablespoon brown sugar
- 1 tablespoon bourbon
- 1 teaspoon dried onion, chopped finely
- ½ tablespoon Worcestershire sauce
- 1 /3 cup spice seasoning

Directions:

1. Stir-cook all the ingredients except the drumsticks for 8-10 minutes in a saucepan.
2. Set aside to cool down.
3. Take Ninja Foodi Grill, arrange it over your kitchen platform, and open the top lid.
4. Arrange the grill grate and close the top lid.
5. Press "GRILL" and select the "MED" grill function. Adjust the timer to 12 minutes and then press "START /STOP." Ninja Foodi will start preheating.
6. Ninja Foodi is preheated and ready to cook when it starts to beep. After you hear a beep, open the top lid.
7. Arrange the drumsticks over the grill grate. Brush with half the sauce.

Nutrition: Calories: 342 Fat: 8.5g Saturated Fat: 1g Trans Fat: 0g Carbohydrates: 10g Fiber: 1.5g Sodium: 319mg Protein: 12.5g

Grilled Chicken Fajitas

Preparation Time: 5 minutes

Cooking Time: 6 minutes

Serving: 6

Ingredients:

CHICKEN

- ¼ cup olive oil, divided
- juice from 1 lime
- 3 large boneless skinless chicken breasts, butterflied
- 1 each red, yellow, and orange peppers
- 1 medium Vidalia onion
- a pinch of salt
- 12 small soft flour tortillas

SEASONING

- 1½ Tbsp. chili powder
- 2 tsp. ground cumin
- 2 tsp. kosher salt

- 2 tsp. smoked paprika
- 1 tsp. ground cinnamon
- 1 tsp. onion powder
- 1 tsp. garlic powder
- 1 tsp. cayenne pepper
- ½ tsp. white sugar
- zest from 1 lime

Directions:

1. Insert the Grill Grate and close the hood. Select GRILL, set the temperature to HIGH, and set the time to 4 minutes. Select START /STOP to begin preheating.
2. Combine all the seasoning ingredients into a small bowl and whisk together.
3. Whisk 2 tablespoons olive oil and the lime juice together in a medium mixing bowl. Add butterflied chicken breasts. Toss to evenly coat.
4. Evenly sprinkle seasoning on both sides of chicken, ensuring uniform coverage.
5. Thinly slice peppers and onion.
6. In a large mixing bowl, toss sliced vegetables with the remaining 2 tablespoons of olive oil and a pinch of salt.

Nutrition: Calories 299 Fat 20 g Protein 52 g

Honey-Mustard Chicken Tenders

Preparation Time: 5 minutes

Cooking Time: 3 minutes

Serving: 4

Ingredients:

- ½ cup Dijon mustard
- 2 tablespoons honey
- 2 tablespoons olive oil
- 1 teaspoon freshly ground black pepper
- 2 pounds chicken tenders
- ½ cup walnuts

Directions:

1. Whisk together the mustard, honey, olive oil, and pepper in a medium bowl. Add the chicken and toss to coat.
2. Finely grind the walnuts by pulsing them in a food processor or putting them in a heavy-duty plastic bag and pounding them with a rolling pin or heavy skillet.
3. Insert the Grill Grate and close the hood. Select GRILL, set the temperature to HIGH, and set the time to 4 minutes. Select START /STOP to begin preheating.

Nutrition: Calories: 444; Fat: 20g; Protein: 5g;

Chicken Roast with Pineapple Salsa

Preparation Time: 10 minutes

Cooking Time: 45 minutes

Serving: 2

Ingredients:

- ¼ cup extra virgin olive oil
- ¼ cup freshly chopped cilantro
- 1 avocado, diced
- 1-pound boneless chicken breasts
- 2 cups canned pineapples
- 2 teaspoons honey
- Juice from 1 lime
- Salt and pepper to taste

Directions:

1. Insert the Crisper Basket, and close the hood. Select AIR CRISP, set the temperature to 390°F, and set the time to 45 minutes. Select START /STOP to begin preheating.
2. Place the grill pan accessory in the air fryer.
3. Season the chicken breasts with lime juice, olive oil, honey, salt, and pepper.

Nutrition: Calories 744 Fat 33 g Protein 5 g Sugar 5 g

Tarragon Chicken Tenders

Preparation Time: 5 minutes

Cooking Time: 5 minutes

Serving: 4

Ingredients:

FOR THE CHICKEN

- 1½ pounds chicken tenders (12 to 16 tenders
- Coarse salt (kosher or sea and freshly ground black pepper
- 3 tablespoons chopped fresh tarragon leaves, plus 4 whole sprigs for garnish
- 1 teaspoon finely grated lemon zest
- 2 tablespoons fresh lemon juice
- 2 tablespoons extra-virgin olive oil

FOR THE SAUCE (OPTIONAL

- 2 tablespoons fresh lemon juice
- 2 tablespoons salted butter
- ½ cup heavy (whipping cream

Directions:

1. Make the chicken: Place the chicken tenders in a nonreactive baking dish just large enough to hold them in a single layer. Season the tenders generously on both sides with salt and pepper. Sprinkle the chopped tarragon and lemon zest all over the tenders, patting them onto the chicken with your fingertips. Drizzle the lemon juice and the olive oil over the tenders and pat them onto the chicken. Let the tenders marinate in the refrigerator, covered, for 10 minutes.
2. Drain the chicken tenders well by lifting one end with tongs and letting the marinade drip off. Discard the marinade.
3. Insert the Grill Grate and close the hood. Select GRILL, set the temperature to HIGH, and set the time

to 4 minutes. Select START /STOP to begin preheating.

Nutrition: Calories 299 Fat 20 g Protein 52 g

Cheesy Chicken in Leek-Tomato Sauce

Preparation Time: 10 minutes

Cooking Time: 20 minutes

Serving: 4

Ingredients:

- 2 large-sized chicken breasts, cut in half lengthwise
- Salt and ground black pepper, to taste
- 4 ounces Cheddar cheese, cut into sticks
- 1 tablespoon sesame oil
- 1 cup leeks, chopped
- 2 cloves garlic, minced
- 2 /3 cup roasted vegetable stock
- 2 /3 cup tomato puree
- 1 teaspoon dried rosemary
- 1 teaspoon dried thyme

Directions:

1. Insert the Crisper Basket, and close the hood. Select AIR CRISP, set the temperature to 390°F, and set the time to 15 minutes. Select START /STOP to begin preheating.
2. Firstly, season chicken breasts with salt and black pepper; place a piece of Cheddar cheese in the middle. Then, tie it using a kitchen string; drizzle with sesame oil, and reserve.
3. Add the leeks and garlic to the oven-safe bowl.

Nutrition: Calories 299 Fat 20 g Protein 52 g

Honey BBQ-Glazed Chicken Drumsticks

Preparation Time: 5 minutes

Cooking Time: 45 minutes

Serving: 5

Ingredients:

- 10 to 12 chicken legs
- 2 Tbsp. baking powder
- ½ Tbsp. kosher salt
- olive oil spray
- 2 Tbsp. BBQ rub, plus 1 tsp. for glaze
- 3 Tbsp. honey

Directions:

1. Remove chicken from its packaging. Rinse and pat dry with a paper towel.
2. Mix baking powder and salt in a shaker bottle and dust over the drumsticks. You want to be sure you coat the skin lightly and evenly; this is essential to dry out the skin, which will allow for the skin to get crispy on the grill.
3. Place chicken in the refrigerator for at least 1 to 2 hours to allow the baking powder and salt to pull the moisture out of the skin.
4. Insert the Grill Grate and close the hood. Select GRILL, set the temperature to HIGH, and set the time to 45 minutes. Select START /STOP to begin preheating.

Nutrition: Calories 299 Fat 20 g Protein 52 g

Mustard Chicken Tenders

Preparation Time: 5 minutes

Cooking Time: 20 minutes

Serving: 4

Ingredients:

- ½ C. coconut flour
- 1 tbsp. spicy brown mustard
- 2 beaten eggs
- 1 pound of chicken tenders

Directions:

1. Insert the Crisper Basket, and close the hood. Select AIR CRISP, set the temperature to 390°F, and set the time to 20 minutes. Select START /STOP to begin preheating.
2. Season tenders with pepper and salt.
3. Place a thin layer of mustard onto tenders and then dredge in flour and dip in egg.

Nutrition: Calories 404 Fat 20 g Protein 22 g Sugar 4 g

BBQ Grilled Chicken

Preparation Time: 5 Minutes

Cooking Time: 30 Minutes

Servings: 4

Ingredients:

- 2 c. barbecue sauce
- Juice of 1 lime
- 2 - tbsp. honey
- 1 - tbsp. hot sauce
- Kosher salt
- Freshly ground black pepper
- 1 lb. boneless skinless chicken breasts
- Vegetable oil, for the grill

Directions:

1. In an enormous bowl, whisk together grill sauce, lime juice, nectar, and hot sauce, and season with salt and pepper. Set aside ½ a cup for seasoning.
2. Add chicken to a bowl and sling until covered.

3. Warmth Ninja Foodi oven broil too high. Oil meshes and Ninja Foodi oven broil chicken, seasoning withheld marinade, until roasted, 8MIN per side for bosoms, and 10 to 12MIN per side for drumsticks.

Nutrition: Calories 180, Fat 6g, carbohydrate 6g, Protein 25g.

Crack BBQ Chicken

Preparation Time: 15 Minutes

Cooking Time: 2 Hours and 30 Minutes

Servings: 8

Ingredients:

- 1 - lb. boneless skinless chicken breasts
- 2 - c. water
- 2 - tbsp. kosher salt
- ¼ - c. brown sugar
- kosher salt
- Freshly ground black pepper
- 1 - c. barbecue sauce
- Juice of 2 limes
- 2 - cloves garlic, Minced

Directions:

1. Set the chook in a bib Ziploc sack and pound until ¼" thick. In a large mixing bowl, whisk collectively water, salt, and sugar until consolidated. Pour the saline answer into Ziploc and refrigerate on any occasion 15MIN, yet preferably 2 HRS.
2. Take the chook out from brackish water and put off fluid.
3. Warmth barbeque to medium. Include chook and season with salt and pepper, at that point Ninja Foodi oven broil 6MIN consistent with aspect.
4. In a medium bowl, whisk together grill sauce, lime juice, and garlic. Treat fowl, flipping sometimes, till caramelized and cooked through.

Nutrition: Calories 122, Fat 11g, carbohydrate 2g, Protein 20g.

Sticky Grilled Chicken

Preparation Time: 10 Minutes

Cooking Time: 2 Hours and 35 Minutes

Servings: 4

Ingredients:

- ½ c. low-sodium soy sauce
- ½ c. balsamic vinegar
- 3 tbsp. honey
- 2 - cloves garlic, Minced
- 2 - green onions, thinly sliced
- 2½ lb. chicken drumsticks
- Vegetable oil, for the grill
- 2 tbsp. sesame seeds, for garnish

Directions:

1. In an enormous bowl, whisk together soy sauce, balsamic vinegar, nectar, garlic, and green onions. Put aside 1/4 cup marinade.
2. Add chicken to an enormous resalable plastic pack and pour it into the outstanding marinade. Let marinate in the cooler at any rate 2 HRS or up to expedite.
3. At the point when prepared to barbecue, heat Ninja Foodi oven broils to high. Oil meshes and barbecue chicken, seasoning with the held marinade and turning each 3 to 4MIN, until sang and cooked through, 24 to 30MIN aggregate.
4. Embellishment with sesame seeds before serving.

Nutrition: Calories 440, Fat 8g, carbohydrate 51g, Protein 40g.

Grilled Chicken Breast

Preparation Time: 15 Minutes

Cooking Time: 45 Minutes

Servings: 4

Ingredients:

- ¼ c. balsamic vinegar
- 3 - tbsp. extra-virgin olive oil
- 2 - tbsp. brown sugar
- 3 - cloves garlic, Minced
- 1 - tsp. dried thyme
- 1 - tsp. dried rosemary
- 4 - chicken breasts
- Kosher salt
- Freshly ground black pepper
- Freshly chopped parsley, for garnish

Directions:

1. In a medium bowl, mix balsamic vinegar, olive oil, earthy colored sugar, garlic, and dried herbs altogether, and season liberally with salt and pepper. Hold ¼ cup.
2. Add a bird to the bowl and hurl to sign up for. Let marinate in any occasion 20MIN and up to expedite.
3. Preheat Ninja Foodi oven broil to medium-high. Include hen and Ninja Foodi oven broil, treating with saved marinade, until cooked through, 6MIN according to facet.
4. Embellishment with parsley earlier than serving.

Nutrition: Calories 208, Fat 4g, carbohydrate 6g, Protein 0g.

Grilled Pineapple Chicken

Preparation Time: 10 Minutes

Cooking Time: 2 Hours and 25 Minutes

Servings: 4

Ingredients:

- 1 c. - unsweetened pineapple juice
- ¾ c. - ketchup
- ½ c. - low-sodium soy sauce
- ½ c. brown sugar
- 2 - cloves garlic, Minced
- 1 - tbsp. freshly Minced ginger
- 1 lb.- boneless skinless chicken breasts
- 1 - tsp. vegetable oil, plus more for the grill
- 1 - pineapple, sliced into rings & halved
- Thinly sliced green onions, for garnish

Directions:

1. In an enormous bowl, whisk together pineapple juice, ketchup, soy sauce, earthy colored sugar, garlic, and ginger until joined.
2. Add chicken to an enormous plastic pack and pour in the marinade. Let marinate in the refrigerator in any event 2 HRS and up to expedite.
3. At the point when prepared to barbecue, heat Ninja Foodi oven broil to high. Oil meshes and Ninja Foodi oven broil chicken, seasoning with marinade until scorched and cooked through, 8MIN per side.
4. Sling pineapple with oil and Ninja Foodi oven broil until burned, 2MIN per side.
5. Topping chicken and pineapple with green onions before serving.

Nutrition: Calories 171, Fat 1g, carbohydrate 12g, Protein 27g.

Grilled Chicken Wings

Preparation Time: 15 Minutes

Cooking Time: 35 Minutes

Servings: 4

Ingredients:

For the wings

- Zest of 1 lemon
- 2 - tsp. kosher salt
- 1 - tsp. smoked paprika
- 1 - tsp. garlic powder
- 1 - tsp. onion powder
- 1 - tsp. dried thyme
- ¼ tsp. cayenne
- 2 lb.- chicken wings
- Vegetable oil, for the grill

For the sauce

- ½ c. mayonnaise
- Juice of 1 lemon
- 1 - tbsp. Dijon mustard
- 2 - tsp. horseradish
- 2 - tsp. freshly chopped chives
- 1 - tsp. hot sauce, such as Crystal

Directions:

1. In a medium bowl, whisk together lemon get-up-and-go, salt, paprika, garlic powder, onion powder, thyme, and cayenne. Pat chicken wings dry and see in a big bowl. Add taste combination and sling to cover.
2. Warm Ninja Foodi oven broil or barbeque dish to medium warm temperature. Oil Ninja Foodi oven broil grates with vegetable oil. Include wings and cook, mixing on occasion, till the skin is fresh and meat is cooked via 15 to 20MIN.
3. In the period in-between, make the sauce: In a medium bowl, whisk collectively mayo, lemon juice, mustard, horseradish, chives, and hot sauce.
4. Serve wings hot with plunging sauce.

Nutrition: Calories 129, Fat 7g, carbohydrate 5g, Protein 10g.

Sweet Chili-Lime Grilled Chicken

Preparation Time: 15 Minutes

Cooking Time: 2 Hours and 25 Minutes

Servings: 4

Ingredients:

- ¾ c. sweet chili sauce
- Juice of 2 limes
- 1 /3 - c. low-sodium soy sauce
- 4 - boneless skinless chicken breasts
- Vegetable oil, for the grill
- Thinly sliced green onions, for garnish
- Lime wedges, for serving

Directions:

1. In an enormous bowl, whisk together bean stew sauce, lime juice, and soy sauce. Put aside 1/4 cup marinade.
2. Add chicken to an enormous plastic sack and pour in the marinade. Let marinate in the cooler at any rate 2 HRS or up to expedite.
3. At the point when prepared to Ninja Foodi oven broil, heat barbecue to high. Oil meshes and Ninja Foodi oven broil chicken, treating with marinade until burned and cooked through, about 8MIN per side.
4. Season with held marinade and enhancement with green onions. Present with lime wedges.

Nutrition: Calories 340, Fat 7g, carbohydrate 41g, Protein 26g.

Honey Balsamic Grilled Chicken Thighs

Preparation Time: 10 Minutes

Cooking Time: 1 Hour and 25 Minutes

Servings: 4

Ingredients:

- 8 - bone-in, skin-on chicken thighs
- Kosher salt
- Freshly ground black pepper

- 2 - tbsp. butter
- 2 - tbsp. balsamic vinegar
- 1/3 - c. honey
- 3 - cloves garlic, peeled and crushed
- Canola oil, for greasing
- Chopped chives, for garnish
- Chopped parsley, for garnish
- Lemon wedges, for garnish

Directions:

1. Spot the chicken thighs on an enormous plate and sprinkle with salt and pepper on all sides. Work the flavoring into the chicken. Let sit, in the fridge, for in any event 60 minutes.

2. Then, make the coating: In a medium pot, soften the spread. Include the vinegar, nectar, and garlic and mix until the nectar has broken down. Season with salt and pepper. Set close to the barbecue.

3. Preheat barbecue to medium-high and clean and oil the meshes with canola oil. Include chicken skin-side-down and Ninja Foodi oven broil, flipping frequently and seasoning with sauce, until cooked through, 10MIN per side.

4. Present with lemon wedges and trimming with chives and parsley

Nutrition: Calories 440, Fat 24g, carbohydrate 35g, Protein 21g.

Pork

Korean Chili Pork

Preparation Time: 5-10 minutes

Cooking Time: 8 minutes

Servings: 4

Ingredients:

- 2 pounds pork, cut into 1/8-inch slices
- 5 minced garlic cloves
- 3 tablespoons minced green onion
- 1 yellow onion, sliced
- ½ cup soy sauce
- ½ cup brown sugar
- 3 tablespoons Korean red chili paste or regular chili paste
- 2 tablespoons sesame seeds
- 3 teaspoons black pepper
- Red pepper flakes to taste

Directions:

1. Take a zip-lock bag, add all the ingredients. Shake well and refrigerate for 6-8 hours to marinate.
2. Take Ninja Foodi Grill, orchestrate it over your kitchen stage, and open the top.
3. Mastermind the barbecue mesh and close the top cover.
4. Click Grill and choose the Med grill function. flame broil work. Modify the clock to 8 minutes and press Start /Stop. Ninja Foodi will begin to warm up.
5. Ninja Foodi is preheated and prepared to cook when it begins to signal. After you hear a signal, open the top.
6. Fix finely sliced pork on the barbeque mesh.
7. Cover and cook for 4 minutes. Then open the cover, switch the side of the pork.
8. Cover it and cook for another 4 minutes.

9. Serve warm with chopped lettuce (optional).

Nutrition: Calories: 621, Fat: 31 g, Saturated Fat: 12.5 g, Trans Fat: 0 g, Carbohydrates: 29 g, Fiber: 3 g, Sodium: 1428 mg, Protein: 53 g

Korean Pork

Preparation Time: 5-10 Minutes

Cooking Time: 8 Minutes

Servings: 4

Ingredients:

- 2 pounds pork, cut into 1/8-inch slices
- 5 minced garlic cloves
- 3 tablespoons minced green onion
- 1 yellow onion, sliced
- ½ cup soy sauce
- ½ cup brown sugar
- 3 tablespoons Korean red chili paste or regular chili paste
- 2 tablespoons sesame seeds
- 3 teaspoons black pepper
- Red pepper flakes to taste

Directions:

1. Take a zip-lock bag, add all the ingredients. Shake well and refrigerate for 6-8 hours to marinate.
2. Take Ninja Foodi Grill, arrange it over your kitchen platform, and open the top lid.
3. Arrange the grill grate and close the top lid.
4. Press "GRILL" and select the "MED" grill function. Adjust the timer to 8 minutes and then press "START /STOP." Ninja Foodi will start preheating.
5. Ninja Foodi is preheated and ready to cook when it starts to beep. After you hear a beep, open the top lid.
6. Arrange the sliced pork over the grill grate.

7. Close the top lid and cook for 4 minutes. Now open the top lid, flip the pork.
8. Close the top lid and cook for 4 more minutes.
9. Serve warm with chopped lettuce, optional.

Nutrition: Calories: 621, Fat: 31g, Saturated Fat: 12.5g, Trans Fat: 0g, Carbohydrates: 29g Fiber: 3g, Sodium: 1428mg, Protein: 53g

Garlic Butter Pork

Preparation Time: 10 minutes

Cooking Time: 20 minutes

Servings: 4

Ingredients:

- 1 tablespoon coconut butter
- 1 tablespoon coconut oil
- 2 teaspoons cloves garlic, grated
- 2 teaspoons parsley
- Salt and pepper to taste
- 4 pork chops, sliced into strips

Directions:

1. Combine all the ingredients except the pork strips. Mix well.
2. Marinate the pork in the mixture for 1 hour. Put the pork on the Ninja Foodi basket.
3. Set it inside the pot. Seal with the crisping lid. Choose Air Crisp.
4. Cook at 400°F for 10 minutes.
5. Serving Suggestion:
6. Serve with a fresh garden salad.

Nutrition: Calories: 388, Total Fat: 23.3 g, Saturated Fat: 10.4 g, Cholesterol: 69 mg, Sodium: 57 mg, Total Carbohydrate: 0.5 g, Dietary Fiber: 0.1 g, Total Sugars: 0 g, Protein: 18.1 g, Potassium: 285 mg

Bourbon Barbecue–Glazed Pork Chops

Preparation Time: 5 Minutes

Cooking Time: 35 Minutes

Servings: 4

Ingredients:

- 2 cups ketchup
- ¾ cup bourbon
- ¼ cup apple cider vinegar
- ¼ cup soy sauce
- 1 cup packed brown sugar
- 3 tablespoons Worcestershire sauce
- ½ tablespoon dry mustard powder
- 4 boneless pork chops
- Sea salt
- Freshly ground black pepper

Directions:

1. In a medium saucepan over high heat, combine the ketchup, bourbon, vinegar, soy sauce, sugar, Worcestershire sauce, and mustard powder. Stir to combine and bring to a boil.
2. Reduce the heat to low and simmer, uncovered and stirring occasionally, for 20 minutes. The barbecue sauce will thicken while cooking. Once thickened, remove the pan from the heat and set it aside.
3. While the barbecue sauce is cooking, insert the Grill Grate into the unit and close the hood. Select GRILL, set the temperature to MEDIUM, and set the time to 15 minutes. Select START /STOP to begin preheating.
4. When the unit beeps to signify it has preheated, place the pork chops on the Grill Grate. Close the hood, and cook for 8 minutes. After 8 minutes, flip the pork chops and baste the cooked side with the barbecue sauce. Close the hood, and cook for 5 minutes more.
5. Open the hood, and flip the pork chops again, basting both sides with the barbecue sauce. Close the hood, and cook for the final 2 minutes.

Nutrition: Calories: 361; Total fat: 14g; Saturated fat: 5g; Cholesterol: 55mg; Sodium: 1412mg; Carbohydrates: 26g; Fiber: 0g; Protein: 26g

Honey-Glazed Pork Tenderloin

Preparation Time: 5 Minutes

Cooking Time: 20 Minutes

Servings: 4

Ingredients:

- 2 tablespoons honey
- 1 tablespoon soy sauce
- ½ teaspoon garlic powder
- ½ teaspoon sea salt
- 1 (1½-pound) pork tenderloin

Directions:

1. Insert the Grill Grate and close the hood. Select GRILL, set the temperature to MEDIUM, and set the time to 20 minutes. Select START /STOP to begin preheating.
2. Meanwhile, in a small bowl, combine the honey, soy sauce, garlic powder, and salt.
3. When the unit beeps to signify it has preheated, place the pork tenderloin on the Grill Grate. Baste all sides with the honey glaze. Close the hood and cook for 8 minutes. After 8 minutes, flip the pork tenderloin and baste with any remaining glaze. Close the hood and cook for 7 minutes more.

Nutrition: Calories: 215; Total fat: 6g; Saturated fat: 2g; Cholesterol: 98mg; Sodium: 558mg; Carbohydrates: 9g; Fiber: 0g; Protein: 30g

Asian Style Pork Ribs

Preparation Time: 5-10 Minutes

Cooking Time: 25 Minutes

Servings: 2

Ingredients:

- ¼ cup hoisin sauce
- ¼ cup hoisin sauce
- 1 teaspoon garlic powder
- 1 teaspoon onion powder
- ¼ cup soy sauce
- ¼ cup apple cider vinegar
- 1-pound pork ribs

Directions:

1 In a mixing bowl, add all the ingredients. Combine the ingredients to mix well with each other.
2 Add the pork ribs and coat well. Refrigerate for 2-4 hours to marinate.
3 Take Ninja Foodi Grill, arrange it over your kitchen platform, and open the top lid.
4 Arrange the grill grate and close the top lid.
5 Press "GRILL" and select the "MED" grill function. Adjust the timer to 24 minutes and then press "START /STOP." Ninja Foodi will start pre-heating.
6 Ninja Foodi is preheated and ready to cook when it starts to beep. After you hear a beep, open the top lid.
7 Arrange the pork ribs over the grill grate.
8 Close the top lid and cook for 12 minutes. Now open the top lid, flip the ribs.
9 Close the top lid and cook for 12 more minutes.
10 Serve warm.

Nutrition: Calories: 326, Fat: 9g, Saturated Fat: 3g, Trans Fat: 0g, Carbohydrates: 26.5g, Fiber: 5g, Sodium: 529mg, Protein: 27g

Creamy Pork Sprouts

Preparation Time: 35Minutes Servings: 4
Cooking Time: 70 Minutes

Ingredients:

- 1-pound Brussels sprouts, halved
- ½ cup heavy cream
- 4 pork chops
- 2 tablespoons avocado oil
- 1 tablespoon coconut aminos
- 1 tablespoon chives, chopped
- A pinch of black pepper (finely ground) and salt

Directions:

1. Take your Ninja Foodi and place it over a dry kitchen platform. Plug it in and open the lid.
2. Pour the oil into the pot. Press "SEAR /SAUTÉ" cooking function. Adjust temperature level to "MD: HI".
3. Press the "START /STOP" button to start the cooking process. It will take 3-5 minutes to pre-heat.
4. When the oil is simmering, add the meat and brown for 4-5 minutes.
5. Add the rest of the ingredients, except the parsley. Stir the mixture using a spatula.
6. Close the top by placing the pressing lid. Do not forget to set the temperature valve in a locked or sealed position.
7. Press the "PRESSURE" cooking function. Adjust and set pressure level to "HI".
8. Adjust cooking time to 20 minutes. Press the "START /STOP" button to start the cooking process.
9. After cooking time is over, allow the build-up pressure to get released for around 10 minutes naturally. Then, set the pressure valve to VENT position to release the remaining pressure quicker.

10. Divide into serving plates or bowls; serve warm topped with some chives.

Nutrition: Calories 368, Fat 19g, Carbohydrates 16g, Fiber 5g, Protein 23g

Green Bean Pork Dinner

Preparation Time: 35 Minutes
Cooking Time: 70 Minutes

Servings: 4

Ingredients:
- 2 garlic cloves, minced
- 1 tablespoon basil, chopped
- 2 pounds pork stew meat, cut into cubes
- 1 tablespoon avocado oil
- 1-pound green beans, trimmed and halved
- 1 teaspoon chili powder
- ¾ cup veggie stock
- A pinch of black pepper (finely ground) and salt

Directions:
1. Take your Ninja Foodi and place it over a dry kitchen platform. Plug it in and open the lid.
2. Pour the oil into the pot. Press "SEAR /SAUTÉ" cooking function. Adjust temperature level to "MD: HI".
3. Press the "START /STOP" button to start the cooking process. It will take 3-5 minutes to pre-heat.
4. When the oil is simmering, add the meat and garlic, stir and cook to evenly brown for 3-4 minutes.
5. Add the remaining ingredients; stir the mixture using a spatula.
6. Close the top by placing the pressing lid. Do not forget to set the temperature valve in a locked or sealed position.
7. Press the "PRESSURE" cooking function. Adjust and set pressure level to "HI".

8. Adjust cooking time to 20 minutes. Press the "START /STOP" button to start the cooking process.
9. After cooking time is over, allow the build-up pressure to get released for around 10 minutes naturally. Then, set the pressure valve to VENT position to release the remaining pressure quicker.
10. Divide into serving plates or bowls; serve warm.

Nutrition: Calories 429, Fat 16g, Carbohydrates 14g, Fiber 4g, Protein 58g

Bourbon Pork Chops

Preparation Time: 5-10 Minutes

Cooking Time: 20 Minutes

Servings: 4

Ingredients:
- 4 boneless pork chops
- Sea salt and ground black pepper to taste
- ¼ cup apple cider vinegar
- ¼ cup soy sauce
- 3 tablespoons Worcestershire sauce
- 2 cups ketchup
- ¾ cup bourbon
- 1 cup packed brown sugar
- ½ tablespoon dry mustard powder

Directions:

1 Take Ninja Foodi Grill, arrange it over your kitchen platform, and open the top lid. Arrange the grill grate and close the top lid.
2 Press "GRILL" and select the "MED" grill function. Adjust the timer to 15 minutes and then press "START /STOP." Ninja Foodi will start preheating.
3 Ninja Foodi is preheated and ready to cook when it starts to beep. After you hear a beep, open the top lid.

4　Arrange the pork chops over the grill grate.

5　Close the top lid and cook for 8 minutes. Now open the top lid, flip the pork chops.

6　Close the top lid and cook for 8 more minutes. Check the pork chops for doneness, cook for 2 more minutes if required.

7　In a saucepan, heat the soy sauce, sugar, ketchup, bourbon, vinegar, Worcestershire sauce, and mustard powder; stir-cook until boils.

8　Reduce heat and simmer for 20 minutes to thicken the sauce.

9　Season the pork chops with salt and black pepper. Serve warm with the prepared sauce.

Nutrition: Calories: 346, Fat: 13.5g, Saturated Fat: 4g, Trans Fat: 0g, Carbohydrates: 27g, Fiber: 0.5g, Sodium: 1324mg, Protein: 27g

Broccoli Pork Meal

Preparation Time: 35-40 Minutes
Cooking Time: 70 Minutes

Servings: 4

Ingredients:
- 2 teaspoons thyme, dried
- 1-pound broccoli florets
- 4 pork chops
- 2 tablespoons avocado oil or vegetable oil
- ½ teaspoon basil, dried
- 1 cup canned tomatoes, drained and chopped
- A pinch of Black pepper (finely-ground) and salt
- 1 tablespoon lime juice

Directions:
1. Take your Ninja Foodi and place it over a dry kitchen platform. Plug it in and open the lid.

2. Pour the oil into the pot. Press "SEAR /SAUTÉ" cooking function. Adjust temperature level to "MD: HI".

3. Press the "START /STOP" button to start the cooking process. It will take 3-5 minutes to pre-heat.

4. When the oil is simmering, add the meat and brown for 5-6 minutes.

5. Add the broccoli and the rest of the ingredients. Stir the mixture.

6. Install the reversible rack in the pot. Place the Crisping Basket into the pot.

7. Close the top by placing the crisping lid. Do not forget to set the pressure valve to a locked position.

8. Press the "AIRCRISP" cooking function. Adjust the temperature level to "390°F".

9. Adjust cooking time to 15 minutes. Press the "START /STOP" button to start the cooking process.

10. After cooking time is over, set the pressure valve to VENT position to release the build-up pressure quicker.

11. Divide into serving plates or bowls; serve warm.

Nutrition: Calories 287, Fat 9g, Carbohydrates 13g, Fiber 4g, Protein 21g

Pork with Gravy

Preparation Time: 10 minutes

Cooking Time: 30minutes

Servings: 4

Ingredients:

- 5 pork chops
- 1 tablespoon olive oil
- 1 teaspoon salt
- ½ teaspoon pepper
- ½ teaspoon garlic powder
- 2 cups beef broth
- 1 packet ranch dressing mix
- 10½ oz. cream of chicken soup
- 1 packet brown gravy mix

- 2 tablespoons corn starch dissolved in 2 tablespoons water

Directions:

1. Season both sides of the pork chops with salt, pepper, and garlic powder.
2. Pour the olive oil into the Ninja Foodi. Set it to Sauté.
3. Brown the pork chops on both sides. Remove and set aside.
4. Pour the beef broth to deglaze the pot.
5. Add the rest of the ingredients except the corn starch. Seal the pot.
6. Set it to Pressure. Cook at high pressure for 8 minutes. Release the pressure naturally.
7. Remove the pork chops. Turn the pot to Sauté. Stir in the corn starch.
8. Simmer to thicken. Pour the gravy over the pork chops.

Nutrition: Calories: 357, Total Fat: 26.8 g, Saturated Fat: 9 g, Cholesterol: 74 mg, Sodium: 1308 mg, Total Carbohydrate: 6 g, Dietary Fiber: 0.1 g, Total Sugars: 0.8 g, Protein: 21.6 g, Potassium: 396 mg

Hawaiian Pork

Preparation Time: 10 minutes

Cooking Time: 20 minutes

Servings: 4

Ingredients:

- 20 oz. pineapple chunks, undrained
- 2 tablespoons water
- 1 tablespoon corn starch
- 2 tablespoons soy sauce
- 3 tablespoons honey
- 1 tablespoon ginger, grated
- 2 tablespoons brown sugar
- 3 cloves garlic, minced
- 2 tablespoons olive oil, divided
- 1 onion, chopped
- 2 lb. pork stew meat
- Salt and pepper to taste

- 1 teaspoon oregano

Directions:

1. Mix the pineapple juice, soy sauce, honey, ginger, sugar, and garlic in a bowl. Set aside. Set the Ninja Foodi to Sauté. Add half of the oil. Cook the onion for 1 minute.
2. Add the remaining oil. Brown the pork on both sides.
3. Add the pineapple chunks, oregano, and pineapple juice mixture.
4. Cover the pot. Set it to Pressure. Cook on high pressure for 10 minutes.
5. Release the pressure naturally.

Nutrition: Calories: 384, Total Fat: 27 g, Saturated Fat: 9 g, Cholesterol: 81 mg, Sodium: 317 mg, Total Carbohydrates: 13 g, Sugars: 10 g, Protein: 20 g, Potassium: 390 mg

Grilled Pork Chops

Preparation Time: 10 minutes

Cooking Time: 15 minutes

Servings: 4

Ingredients:

- 4 pork chops
- Barbecue sauce
- Salt and pepper to taste

Directions:

1. Add grill grate to your Ninja Foodi Grill.
2. Set it to grill. Close the hood.
3. Preheat to high for 15 minutes.
4. Season pork chops with salt and pepper.
5. Add to the grill grates.
6. Grill for 8 minutes.
7. Flip and cook for another 7 minutes, brushing both sides with barbecue sauce.

Nutrition: Calories 368, Fat 19g, Carbohydrates 16g, Fiber 5g, Protein 23g

Cuban Pork Chops

Preparation Time: 8 hours and 20 minutes

Cooking Time: 30 minutes

Servings: 4

Ingredients:

- 4 pork chops
- 1 /2 cup olive oil
- 1 /2 cup lime juice
- 1 teaspoon orange zest
- 8 cloves garlic, minced
- 1 /4 cup mint leaves, chopped
- 2 teaspoons dried oregano
- 1 cup orange juice
- 1 teaspoon lime zest
- 2 teaspoons ground cumin
- 1 cup cilantro, chopped

Directions:

1. Place pork chops on a shallow plate.
2. In another bowl, mix the remaining ingredients.
3. Take ¼ cup of the mixture and set aside.
4. Add the remaining mixture to the pork chops.
5. Cover and marinate in the refrigerator for 8 hours.
6. Add grill grate to the Ninja Foodi Grill. Seal the hood.
7. Choose the grill setting.
8. Set it to high.
9. Set the time to 15 minutes.
10. Close the hood and cook for 15 minutes, flipping once.

Nutrition: Calories 368, Fat 19g, Carbohydrates 16g, Fiber 5g, Protein 23g

Ranch Pork Chops

Preparation Time: 20 minutes

Cooking Time: 20 minutes

Servings: 4

Ingredients:

- 1 teaspoon garlic powder
- 1 tablespoon Parmesan cheese, grated
- 1 /2 cup ranch dressing
- Salt and pepper to taste
- 1 cup breadcrumbs
- 1 tablespoon buttermilk
- 4 pork chops

Directions:

1. Mix garlic powder, breadcrumbs, Parmesan cheese, salt, and pepper in a bowl.
2. Combine buttermilk and ranch dressing in another wall.
3. Dip the pork chops in the buttermilk mixture.
4. Dredge with the breadcrumb mixture.
5. Set the Ninja Foodi Grill to air fry.
6. Cook at 330 degrees F for 10 minutes per side.

Nutrition: Calories 368, Fat 19g, Carbohydrates 16g, Fiber 5g, Protein 23g

Chili Pork Ribs

Preparation Time: 5-10 Minutes

Cooking Time: 60 Minutes

Servings: 6

Ingredients:

Sauce:

- ½ cup of soy sauce
- 1 /6 cup lemon juice

- ½ cup packed brown sugar
- 1 /3 cup ketchup
- 3 /4 teaspoons minced gingerroot

Ribs:

- 3 pounds pork baby back ribs
- 1 tablespoon chili powder
- 1 teaspoon garlic powder
- 1 ½ teaspoon cumin, ground
- 1 tablespoon paprika powder
- Salt to taste
- 1 ½ tablespoons sugar, brown

Directions:

1. In a mixing bowl, add the spices and sugar. Combine the ingredients to mix well with each other.
2. Add the ribs and rub evenly. Cover and refrigerate for about 1 hour to marinate.
3. In a saucepan, heat all the sauce ingredients for about 8 minutes. Set aside.
4. Take Ninja Foodi Grill, arrange it over your kitchen platform, and open the top lid.
5. Arrange the grill grate and close the top lid.
6. Press "GRILL" and select the "HIGH" grill function. Adjust the timer to 45 minutes and then press "START /STOP." Ninja Foodi will start pre-heating.
7. Ninja Foodi is preheated and ready to cook when it starts to beep. After you hear a beep, open the top lid. Arrange the ribs over the grill grate.
8. Close the top lid and cook for 10 minutes. Now open the top lid, flip the ribs. Close the top lid and cook for ten more minutes. Keep flipping every 10 minutes.
9. Serve warm with the prepared sauce.

Nutrition: Calories: 362, Fat: 19g, Saturated Fat: 4.5g, Trans Fat: 0g, Carbohydrates: 32.5g, Fiber: 1.5g, Sodium: 625mg, Protein: 22g

Breaded Pork Chop

Preparation Time: 7 minutes

Cooking Time 12 minutes

Servings: 4

Ingredients:

- 4 5-oz ¾" boneless pork chops, fat trimmed
- ½ cup panko bread crumbs
- 2 tbsp. parmesan cheese, grated
- egg, beaten
- 1 tsp paprika
- ½ tsp garlic powder
- ½ tsp onion powder
- Salt and pepper to taste

Directions:

1. Preheat the Ninja Air Fryer to 400 degrees F and spray the air fryer basket with nonstick spray.
2. Combine the panko bread crumbs, parmesan cheese, salt, pepper, onion, powder, garlic powder, and paprika in a shallow bowl large enough to fit the pork chops.
3. Place the egg in another bowl of the same size.
4. Dip the pork chops into the egg and coat then the panko mixture
5. Place the pork chops into the air fryer and cook for 12 minutes. Flip halfway through the process. Serve with your favorite sides.

Nutrition: Calories: 304 kcal, Carbs: 11.7g, Fat: 15.6 g, Protein: 29.5 g.

Italian Herb Pork Chops

Preparation Time: 4 minutes

Cooking Time 12 minutes

Servings: 2

Ingredients:

- 2 1" thick pork chops
- ½ tbsp. Italian seasoning
- 2 tbsp. olive oil

Directions:

1. Combine all the ingredients and allow to marinate in a sealed plastic bag for at least 2 hours.
2. Preheat the air fryer to 350 degrees.
3. Place the pork chops in the air fryer basket and cook for 12 minutes. Flip halfway through the cooking process.
4. Allow the pork chops to sit for at least 5 minutes before serving.

Nutrition: Calories: 387 kcal, Carbs: 0.4 g, Fat: 34.9 g, Protein: 18 g.

Italian Stuffed Pork Chops

Preparation Time: 10 minutes

Cooking Time 12 minutes

Servings: 4

Ingredients:

- 4 thick-cut pork chops
- 4 tbsp. cream cheese
- 1 cup spinach
- ½ cup mozzarella cheese
- ½ tbsp. dried rosemary
- ½ tbsp. dried oregano
- ½ tbsp. garlic powder
- ½ tbsp. onion powder
- 1 tsp paprika
- Salt and pepper to taste

Directions:

1. Preheat the Ninja Air Fryer to 400 degrees F.
2. Butterfly the pork chops using a sharp knife. Season with salt and pepper.
3. Add all the remaining ingredients to a small bowl and combine thoroughly.
4. Fill each pork chop with an equal amount of filling.
5. Place the pork chops filling side up in the air fryer and cook for up to 12 minutes. Serve with the desired sides.

Nutrition: Calories: 378 kcal, Carbs: 3.1 g, Fat: 19.4 g, Protein: 23.4 g.

Beef

Roast Beef with Garlic

Preparation Time: 15 minutes

Cooking Time: 1 hour and 20 minutes

Servings: 4

Ingredients:

- 2 lb. beef roast, sliced
- 2 tablespoons vegetable oil
- Salt and pepper to taste
- 6 cloves garlic

Directions:

1. Coat beef roast with oil.
2. Season with salt and pepper.
3. Place them inside the Ninja Foodi Grill pot.
4. Sprinkle garlic on top.
5. Choose the Bake setting.
6. Set it to 400°F and cook for 30 minutes.
7. Reduce the temperature to 375°F and cook for another 40 minutes.

Serving Suggestions: Serve with mashed potato and gravy.

Preparation /Cooking Tips: If refrigerated, let beef come to room temperature 2 hours before cooking.

Nutrition: Calories: 390, Fat: 29 g, Carbohydrates: 5 g, Protein: 20 g

Grilled Steak & Potatoes

Preparation Time: 20 minutes

Cooking Time: 50 minutes

Servings: 4

Ingredients:

- 4 potatoes
- 3 sirloin steaks
- ¼ cup avocado oil
- 2 tablespoons steak seasoning
- Salt to taste

Directions:

1. Poke potatoes with a fork.
2. Coat potatoes with half of the avocado oil.
3. Season with salt.
4. Add to the air fryer basket.
5. Choose the air fry function in your Ninja Foodi Grill.
6. Seal the hood and cook at 400°F for 35 minutes.
7. Flip and cook for another 10 minutes.
8. Transfer to a plate.
9. Add the grill grate to the Ninja Foodi Grill.
10. Add steaks to the grill grate.
11. Set it to High.
12. Cook for 7 minutes per side.
13. Serve steaks with potatoes.

Serving Suggestions: Serve with steak sauce and hot sauce.

Preparation /Cooking Tips: Press steaks onto the grill to give it grill marks.

Nutrition: Calories: 245, Fat: 26 g, Carbohydrates: 7 g, Protein: 19 g

Cooking Time: 10minutes

Servings: 4

Ingredients:

- 1 teaspoon red pepper flakes
- ½ cup and 1 tablespoon soy sauce
- 1½ pounds flank steak
- ¼ cup and 2 tablespoons vegetable oil
- ½ cup of rice wine vinegar
- 3 tablespoons sriracha
- 2 cucumbers, seeded and sliced
- 4 garlic cloves, minced
- 2 tablespoons ginger, minced
- 2 tablespoons honey
- 3 tablespoons sesame oil
- 1 teaspoon sugar
- Salt to taste

Directions:

1. Take a bowl and add ½ cup soy sauce, half of the rice wine, honey, ginger, garlic, 2 tablespoons sriracha, 2 tablespoons sesame oil, and vegetable oil.
2. Mix well, pour half of the mixture over the steak, and rub well.
3. Cover steak and let it sit for 10 minutes.
4. Prepare the salad mix by add remaining rice wine vinegar, sesame oil, sugar red pepper flakes, sriracha sauce, soy sauce, and salt in a salad bowl.
5. Preheat your Ninja Foodi Grill on High, with the timer set to 12 minutes.
6. Transfer steak to your Grill and cook for 6 minutes per side.
7. Slice and serve with the salad mix.
8. Enjoy!

Nutrition: Calories: 327, Fat: 4 g, Saturated Fat: 0.5 g, Carbohydrates: 33 g, Fiber: 1 g, Sodium: 142 mg, Protein: 24 g

Authentic Korean Flank Steak

Preparation Time: 10 minutes

Grilled Beef Burgers

Preparation Time: 5-10 Minutes

Cooking Time: 10 Minutes

Servings: 4

Ingredients:

- 4 ounces cream cheese
- 4 slices bacon, cooked and crumbled
- 2 seeded jalapeño peppers, stemmed, and minced
- ½ cup shredded Cheddar cheese
- ½ teaspoon chili powder
- ¼ teaspoon paprika
- ¼ teaspoon ground black pepper
- 2 pounds ground beef
- 4 hamburger buns
- 4 slices pepper Jack cheese
- Optional - Lettuce, sliced tomato, and sliced red onion

Directions:

1. In a mixing bowl, combine the peppers, Cheddar cheese, cream cheese, and bacon until well combined.
2. Prepare the ground beef into 8 patties. Add the cheese mixture onto four of the patties; arrange a second patty on top of each to prepare four burgers. Press gently.
3. In another bowl, combine the chili powder, paprika, and pepper. Sprinkle the mixture onto the sides of the burgers.
4. Take Ninja Foodi Grill, arrange it over your kitchen platform, and open the top lid.
5. Arrange the grill grate and close the top lid.
6. Press "GRILL" and select the "HIGH" grill function. Adjust the timer to 4 minutes and then press "START /STOP." Ninja Foodi will start pre-heating.
7. Ninja Foodi is preheated and ready to cook when it starts to beep. After you hear a beep, open the top lid.
8. Arrange the burgers over the grill grate.

9. Close the top lid and allow it to cook until the timer reads zero. Cook for 3-4 more minutes, if needed.
10. Cook until the food thermometer reaches 145°F. Serve warm.
11. Serve warm with buns. Add your choice of toppings: pepper Jack cheese, lettuce, tomato, and red onion.

Nutrition: Calories: 783, Fat: 38g, Saturated Fat: 16g, Trans Fat: 0g, Carbohydrates: 25g, Fiber: 3g, Sodium: 1259mg, Protein: 57.5g

Generous Pesto Beef Meal

Preparation Time: 10 minutes

Cooking Time: 14 minutes

Servings: 4

Ingredients:

- ½ teaspoon pepper
- ½ teaspoon salt
- ½ cup feta cheese, crumbled
- 2 /3 cup pesto
- ½ cup walnuts, chopped
- 4 cups grape tomatoes, halved
- 4 cups penne pasta, uncooked
- 10 ounces baby spinach, chopped
- 4 beef (6 ounces each) tenderloin steaks

Directions:

1. Cook the pasta according to the package Directions.
2. Drain the pasta and rinse it.
3. Keep the pasta on the side.
4. Season the tenderloin steaks with pepper and salt.
5. Preheat your Ninja Foodi Grill to High and set the timer to 7 minutes.
6. You will hear a beep once the preheating sequence is complete.
7. Transfer steak to your grill and cook for 7 minutes, flip and cook for 7 minutes more.

84

8. Take a bowl and add pasta, walnuts, spinach, tomatoes, and pesto.
9. Mix well.
10. Garnish your steak with cheese and serve with the prepared sauce.
11. Enjoy!

Nutrition: Calories: 361, Fat: 5 g, Saturated Fat: 1 g, Carbohydrates: 16 g, Fiber: 4 g, Sodium: 269 mg, Protein: 33 g

Meatball Sandwiches with Mozzarella and Basil

Preparation Time: 5 Minutes

Cooking Time: 10 Minutes

Servings: 4

Ingredients:

- 12 frozen meatballs
- 8 slices mozzarella cheese
- 4 sub rolls, halved lengthwise
- ½ cup marinara sauce, warmed
- 12 fresh basil leaves

Directions:

1. Insert the Crisper Basket and close the hood. Select AIR CRISP, set the temperature to 350°F, and set the time to 10 minutes. Select START /STOP to begin preheating.
2. When the unit beeps to signify it has preheated, place the meatballs in the basket. Close the hood and cook for 5 minutes.
3. After 5 minutes, shake the basket of meatballs. Place the basket back in the unit and close the hood to resume cooking.
4. While the meatballs are cooking, place two slices of mozzarella cheese on each sub roll. Use a spoon to spread the marinara sauce on top of the cheese slices. Press three leaves of basil into the sauce on each roll.

Nutrition: Calories: 537; Total fat: 27g; Saturated fat: 13g; Cholesterol: 80mg; Sodium: 1243mg; Carbohydrates: 46g; Fiber: 4g; Protein: 34g

Soy and Garlic Steak Kebabs

Preparation Time: 5 Minutes

Cooking Time: 12 Minutes

Servings: 4

Ingredients:

- ¾ cup soy sauce
- 5 garlic cloves, minced
- 3 tablespoons sesame oil
- ½ cup canola oil
- 1/3 cup sugar
- ¼ teaspoon dried ground ginger
- 2 (10- to 12-ounce) New York strip steaks, cut in 2-inch cubes
- 1 cup whole white mushrooms
- 1 red bell pepper, seeded, and cut into 2-inch cubes
- 1 red onion, cut into 2-inch wedges

Directions:

1. In a medium bowl, whisk together the soy sauce, garlic, sesame oil, canola oil, sugar, and ginger until well combined. Add the steak and toss to coat. Cover and refrigerate for at least 30 minutes.
2. Insert the Grill Grate and close the hood. Select GRILL, set the temperature to MEDIUM, and set the time to 12 minutes. Select START /STOP to begin preheating.
3. While the unit is preheating, assemble the skewers in the following order: steak, mushroom, bell pepper, onion. Ensure the ingredients are pushed almost completely down to the end of the skewers.
4. When the unit beeps to signify it has preheated, place the skewers on the

Grill Grate. Close the hood and cook for 8 minutes without flipping.

5. After 8 minutes, check the steak for the desired doneness, cooking up to 4 minutes more if desired.

Nutrition: Calories: 647; Total fat: 45g; Saturated fat: 12g; Cholesterol: 135mg; Sodium: 1001mg; Carbohydrates: 17g; Fiber: 1g; Protein: 47g

Chili-Rubbed Flank Steak

Preparation Time: 10 Minutes

Cooking Time: 8 Minutes

Servings: 2

Ingredients:

- 1 tablespoon chili powder
- 1 teaspoon dried oregano
- 2 teaspoons ground cumin
- 1 teaspoon sea salt
- ¼ teaspoon freshly ground black pepper
- 2 (8-ounce) flank steaks

Directions:

1. Insert the Grill Grate and close the hood. Select GRILL, set the temperature to HIGH, and set the time to 8 minutes. Select START /STOP to begin preheating.
2. In a small bowl, mix the chili powder, oregano, cumin, salt, and pepper. Use your hands to rub the spice mixture on all sides of the steaks.
3. When the unit beeps to signify it has preheated, place the steaks on the Grill Grate. Gently press the steaks down to maximize grill marks. Close the hood and cook for 4 minutes. After 4 minutes, flip the steaks, close the hood, and cook for 4 minutes more.
4. Remove the steaks from the grill, and transfer them to a cutting board. Let

rest for 5 minutes before slicing and serving.

Nutrition: Calories: 363; Total fat: 15g; Saturated fat: 6g; Cholesterol: 100mg; Sodium: 1008mg; Carbohydrates: 4g; Fiber: 2g; Protein: 51g

Beef Bulgogi

Preparation Time: 5 Minutes

Cooking Time: 5 Minutes

Servings: 4

Ingredients:

- 1/3 cup soy sauce
- 2 tablespoons sesame oil
- 2½ tablespoons brown sugar
- 3 garlic cloves, minced
- ½ teaspoon freshly ground black pepper
- 1-pound rib-eye steak, thinly sliced
- 2 scallions, thinly sliced, for garnish
- Toasted sesame seeds, for garnish

Directions:

1. In a small bowl, whisk together the soy sauce, sesame oil, brown sugar, garlic, and black pepper until fully combined.
2. Place the beef into a large shallow bowl, and pour the sauce over the slices. Cover and refrigerate for 1 hour.
3. Insert the Grill Grate and close the hood. Select GRILL, set the temperature to MEDIUM, and set the time to 5 minutes. Select START /STOP to begin preheating.
4. When the unit beeps to signify it has preheated, place the beef onto the Grill Grate. Close the hood and cook for 4 minutes without flipping.
5. After 4 minutes, check the steak for the desired doneness, cooking for up to 1 minute more if desired.

Nutrition: Calories: 403; Total fat: 31g; Saturated fat: 13g; Cholesterol: 76mg; Sodium: 1263mg; Carbohydrates: 8g; Fiber: 0g; Protein: 22g

Kale Sausage Soup

Preparation Time: 5-10 Minutes

Cooking Time: 10 Minutes

Servings: 4

Ingredients:

- ½ diced onion
- 2 cups chicken broth
- 1-pound chopped sausage roll
- 1 tablespoon olive oil
- 2 cup almond milk
- ½ cup parmesan cheese
- 3 cups chopped kale fresh
- 28-ounce tomatoes, crushed
- 1 tablespoon minced garlic
- 1 teaspoon oregano, dried
- ¼ teaspoon salt

Directions:

1. Take Ninja Foodi multi-cooker, arrange it over a cooking platform, and open the top lid.
2. Select "SEAR /SAUTÉ" mode and select "MD: HI" pressure level. Press "STOP /START." After about 4-5 minutes, the unit is ready to cook.
3. Add the sausage and stir-cook to brown evenly. Add the spices, onions, kale, tomatoes, milk, and chicken broth. Stir the mixture.
4. Seal the multi-cooker by locking it with the pressure lid; ensure to keep the pressure release valve locked /sealed.
5. Select the "PRESSURE" mode and select the "HI" pressure level. Then, set the timer to 10 minutes and press "STOP /START"; it will start the cooking process by building up inside pressure.

6. When the timer goes off, naturally release inside pressure for about 8-10 minutes. Then, quick-release pressure by adjusting the pressure valve to the VENT. Serve warm with the cheese on top and enjoy!

Nutrition: Calories: 162, Fat: 10.5g, Saturated Fat: 4g, Trans Fat: 0g, Carbohydrates: 2g, Fiber: 0.5g, Sodium: 624mg, Protein: 19g

Kale Beef Congee

Preparation Time: 50-60 Minutes
Cooking Time: 70 Minutes

Servings: 5-6

Ingredients:
- 2 cloves garlic, minced
- 6 cups beef stock
- 2 pounds ground beef
- (1 inch) piece fresh ginger, minced
- 1 cup jasmine rice, uncooked, rinsed, and drained
- 1 cup kale, roughly chopped
- 1 cup of water
- Ground black pepper and salt to taste
- Fresh cilantro, chopped

Directions:
1. Take your Ninja Foodi and place it over a dry kitchen platform. Plug it in and open the lid.
2. Add the garlic, rice, and ginger into the cooking pot
3. Pour the stock and water. Stir the mixture using a spatula. Add the beef on top.
4. Close the top by placing the pressing lid. Do not forget to set the temperature valve in a locked or sealed position.
5. Press the "PRESSURE" cooking function. Adjust and set pressure level to "HI".

6. Adjust cooking time to 30 minutes. Press the "START /STOP" button to start the cooking process.
7. After cooking time is over, allow the build-up pressure to get released for around 10 minutes naturally. Then, set the pressure valve to VENT position to release the remaining pressure quicker.
8. Stir in the kale. Season with pepper and salt. Mix everything one more time
9. Divide into serving plates or bowls; serve warm topped with some cilantro.

Nutrition: Calories 334, Fat 16g, Carbohydrates 10g, Fiber 2g, Protein 36g

Grilled Steak Salad with Blue Cheese Dressing

Preparation Time: 5 Minutes

Cooking Time: 16 Minutes

Servings: 4 to 6

Ingredients:

- 4 (8-ounce) skirt steaks
- Sea salt
- Freshly ground black pepper
- 6 cups chopped romaine lettuce
- ¾ cup cherry tomatoes halved
- ¼ cup blue cheese, crumbled
- 1 cup croutons
- 2 avocados, peeled and sliced
- 1 cup blue cheese dressing

Directions:

1. Insert the Grill Grate and close the hood. Select GRILL, set the temperature to HIGH, and set the time to 8 minutes. Select START /STOP to begin preheating.
2. Season the steaks on both sides with salt and pepper.
3. When the unit beeps to signify it has preheated, place 2 steaks on the Grill Grate. Gently press the steaks down to

maximize grill marks. Close the hood and cook for 4 minutes. After 4 minutes, flip the steaks, close the hood, and cook for an additional 4 minutes.
4. Remove the steaks from the grill and transfer to them a cutting board. Tent with aluminum foil.
5. Repeat step 3 with the remaining 2 steaks.

Nutrition: Calories: 911; Total fat: 67g; Saturated fat: 18g; Cholesterol: 167mg; Sodium: 1062mg; Carbohydrates: 22g; Fiber: 7g; Protein: 56g

Meatloaf

Preparation Time: 5-10 Minutes

Cooking Time: 22 Minutes

Servings: 5-6

Ingredients:

- 1-pound ground beef
- 1 tablespoon tomato paste
- 8 ounces Parmesan cheese, grated
- 3 eggs
- 4 tablespoons butter
- 1 tablespoon coconut flour
- 1 teaspoon ground black pepper
- 1 tablespoon salt
- 1 large onion, chopped
- 1 teaspoon minced garlic
- 1 teaspoon cilantro
- 2 tablespoons olive oil

Directions:

1. Add the onion to the blender and puree until smooth.
2. In a mixing bowl, combine the pureed onion, ground black pepper, salt, tomato paste, minced garlic, coconut flour, and cilantro. Add the ground beef and combine well.
3. In a mixing bowl, beat the eggs. Add with the beef mixture and combine to

make a loaf shape. Wrap it in aluminum foil.

4. Take Ninja Foodi multi-cooker, arrange it over a cooking platform, and open the top lid. In the pot, add water and arrange a reversible rack; place the meatloaf over the rack. Seal the multi-cooker by locking it with the pressure lid; ensure to keep the pressure release valve locked /sealed.

5. Select the "STEAM" mode and select the "HI" pressure level. Then, set the timer to 20 minutes and press "STOP /START"; it will start the cooking process by building up inside pressure.

6. When the timer goes off, quick release pressure by adjusting the pressure valve to the VENT. After pressure gets released, open the pressure lid. Remove the foil and add the cheese on top. Add it back in the pot.

7. Seal the multi-cooker by locking it with the pressure lid; ensure to keep the pressure release valve locked /sealed.

8. Select "PRESSURE" mode and select the "HI" pressure level. Then, set the timer to 2 minutes and press "STOP /START"; it will start the cooking process by building up inside pressure.

9. When the timer goes off, quick release pressure by adjusting the pressure valve to the VENT. After pressure gets released, open the pressure lid. Serve warm and enjoy!

Nutrition: Calories: 418, Fat: 28.5g, Saturated Fat: 4g, Trans Fat: 0g, Carbohydrates: 5g, Fiber: 1.5g, Sodium: 786mg, Protein: 38g

Asparagus Tomato Beef

Preparation Time: 35-40 Minutes
Cooking Time: 70 Minutes

Servings: 4

Ingredients:
- ½ pound asparagus, trimmed, steamed, and halved
- cup tomato puree
- 1-pound beef stew meat, cut into cubes
- tablespoons ginger, grated
- A pinch of black pepper (finely ground) and salt
- 1 yellow onion, chopped
- 1 tablespoon olive oil

Directions:
1. Take your Ninja Foodi and place it over a dry kitchen platform. Plug it in and open the lid.
2. Pour the oil into the pot. Press "SEAR /SAUTÉ" cooking function. Adjust temperature level to "MD: HI".
3. Press the "START /STOP" button to start the cooking process. It will take 3-5 minutes to pre-heat.
4. When the oil is simmering, add the meat and brown for 4-5 minutes.
5. Add the onion, ginger, black pepper, and salt; stir and cook for 4 minutes more.
6. Mix in the tomato puree; stir the mixture using a spatula.
7. Close the top by placing the pressing lid. Do not forget to set the temperature valve in a locked or sealed position.
8. Press the "PRESSURE" cooking function. Adjust and set pressure level to "HI".
9. Adjust cooking time to 15 minutes. Press the "START /STOP" button to start the cooking process.
10. After cooking time is over, allow the build-up pressure to get released for around 10 minutes naturally. Then, set the pressure valve to VENT position to release the remaining pressure quicker.
11. Open the lid; mix in the asparagus.
12. Press the "SEAR /SAUTÉ" cooking function. Adjust temperature level to "MD: HI". Stir and cook for 4-5 minutes.
13. Divide into serving plates or bowls; serve warm.

Nutrition: Calories 273, Fat 11g, Carbohydrates 8g, Fiber 2g, Protein 36g

Beef Meatloaf with Spinach

Preparation Time: 5-10 Minutes

Cooking Time: 70 Minutes

Servings: 6

Ingredients:

- ¼ cup tomato puree or crushed tomatoes
- 1-pound lean ground beef
- ½ cup onion, chopped
- 2 garlic cloves, minced
- ½ cup green bell pepper, seeded and chopped
- 2 eggs, beaten
- 1 cup cheddar cheese, grated
- 3 cups spinach, chopped
- 1 teaspoon dried thyme, crushed
- 6 cups mozzarella cheese, grated
- Black pepper to taste

Directions:

1. Take a baking pan; grease it with some cooking spray, vegetable oil, or butter. Take Ninja Foodi multi-cooker, arrange it over a cooking platform, and open the top lid.
2. In a mixing bowl, add all the listed ingredients except cheese and spinach.
3. Place the mixture over a wax paper; top with spinach, cheese, and roll it to form a nice meatloaf. Remove wax paper and add the mixture to the baking pan.
4. In the pot, add water and place a reversible rack inside the pot. Place the pan over the rack.
5. Seal the multi-cooker by locking it with the crisping lid; ensure to keep the pressure release valve locked /sealed.
6. Select "BAKE /ROAST" mode and adjust the 380°F temperature level. Then, set the timer to 70 minutes and press "STOP /START"; it will start the

cooking process by building up inside pressure.
7. When the timer goes off, quick release pressure by adjusting the pressure valve to the VENT. After pressure gets released, open the pressure lid.
8. Serve warm.

Nutrition: Calories: 426, Fat: 16.5g, Saturated Fat: 2g, Trans Fat: 0g, Carbohydrates: 5.5g, Fiber: 1g, Sodium: 743mg, Protein: 48.5g

Beef Sirloin Roast

Preparation Time: 10 minutes

Cooking Time: 50 minutes

Servings: 8

Ingredients:

tablespoon smoked paprika

- 1 teaspoon ground cumin
- 1 teaspoon garlic powder
- Salt and ground black pepper, as required
- 2½ pounds sirloin roast

Direction:

1. In a bowl, mix the spices, salt, and black pepper.
2. Rub the roast with spice mixture generously.
3. Place the sirloin roast into the greased baking pan.
4. Press the "Power Button" of Ninja Foodi Digital Air Fry Oven and turn the dial to select the "Air Roast" mode.
5. Press the Time button and again turn the dial to set the cooking time to 50 minutes.
6. Now push the Temp button and rotate the dial to set the temperature at 350 degrees F.
7. Press the "Start /Pause" button to start.

8. When the unit beeps to show that it is preheated, open the lid and insert the baking pan in the oven.
9. Remove the baking pan from the oven and place the roast onto a platter for about 10 minutes before slicing.
10. With a sharp knife, cut the beef roast into desired sized slices and serve.

Nutrition: Calories 260, Total Fat 11.9 g, Saturated Fat 4.4 g, Cholesterol 101 mg, Sodium 98 mg, Total Carbs 0.4 g, Fiber 0.1 g, Sugar 0.1 g, Protein 38 g

Simple Beef Tenderloin

Preparation Time: 10 minutes

Cooking Time: 50 minutes

Servings: 10

Ingredients:

- 1 (3½-pound) beef tenderloin, trimmed
- 2 tablespoons olive oil
- Salt and ground black pepper, as required

Direction:

1. With kitchen twine, tie the tenderloin.
2. Rub the tenderloin with oil and season with salt and black pepper.
3. Place the tenderloin into the greased baking pan.
4. Press the "Power Button" of Ninja Foodi Digital Air Fry Oven and turn the dial to select the "Air Roast" mode.
5. Press the Time button and again turn the dial to set the cooking time to 50 minutes.
6. Now push the Temp button and rotate the dial to set the temperature at 400 degrees F.
7. Press the "Start /Pause" button to start.
8. When the unit beeps to show that it is preheated, open lid and insert the baking pan in the oven.

9. Remove from the oven and place the tenderloin onto a platter for about 10 minutes before slicing.
10. With a sharp knife, cut the tenderloin into desired sized slices and serve.

Nutrition: Calories 351, Total Fat 17.3 g, Saturated Fat 5.9 g, Cholesterol 146 mg, Sodium 109 mg, Total Carbs 0 g, Fiber 0 g, Sugar 0 g, Protein 46 g

Beef Chuck Roast

Preparation Time: 10 minutes

Cooking Time: 45 minutes

Servings: 6

Ingredients:

- 1 (2-pound) beef chuck roast
- 1 tablespoon olive oil
- 1 teaspoon dried rosemary, crushed
- 1 teaspoon dried thyme, crushed
- Salt, as required

Direction:

1. In a bowl, add the oil, herbs, and salt and mix well.
2. Coat the beef roast with herb mixture generously.
3. Arrange the beef roast onto the greased cooking pan.
4. Press the "Power Button" of Ninja Foodi Digital Air Fry Oven and turn the dial to select the "Air Fry" mode.
5. Press the Time button and again turn the dial to set the cooking time to 45 minutes.
6. Now push the Temp button and rotate the dial to set the temperature at 360 degrees F.
7. Press the "Start /Pause" button to start.
8. When the unit beeps to show that it is preheated, open the lid and insert the baking pan in the oven.

9. Remove from the oven and place the roast onto a cutting board.
10. With a piece of foil, cover the beef roast for about 20 minutes before slicing.
11. With a sharp knife, cut the beef roast into desired size slices and serve.

Nutrition: Calories 304, Total Fat 14 g, Saturated Fat 4.5 g, Cholesterol 130 mg, Sodium 82 mg, Total Carbs 0.2g, Fiber 0.2 g, Sugar 0 g, Protein 41.5 g

Spiced Flank Steak

Preparation Time: 15 minutes

Cooking Time: 12 minutes

Servings: 6

Ingredients:

- 2 tablespoons balsamic vinegar
- 2 tablespoons olive oil
- 3 garlic cloves, minced
- 1 teaspoon red chili powder
- 1 teaspoon ground cumin
- 1 teaspoon onion powder
- Salt and ground black pepper, as required
- 1 (2-pound) flank steak

Direction:

1. In a large bowl, mix the vinegar, spices, salt, and black pepper.
2. Add the steak and coat with mixture generously.
3. Cover the bowl and place it in the refrigerator for at least 1 hour.
4. Remove the steak from the bowl and place it onto the greased "Sheet Pan".
5. Press the "Power Button" of Ninja Foodi Digital Air Fry Oven and turn the dial to select the "Air Broil" mode.
6. Press the Time button and again turn the dial to set the cooking time to 12 minutes.
7. Press the "Start /Pause" button to start.

8. When the unit beeps to show that it is preheated, open the lid.
9. Insert the "Sheet Pan" in the oven.
10. Flip the steak once halfway through.
11. Remove from the oven and place the steak onto a cutting board.
12. With a sharp knife, cut the steak into desired sized slices and serve.

Nutrition: Calories 341, Total Fat 17.4 g, Saturated Fat 5.9 g, Cholesterol 83 mg, Sodium 117 mg, Total Carbs 1.3 g, Fiber 0.2 g, Sugar 0.2 g, Protein 42.3 g

Buttered Rib Eye Steak

Preparation Time: 15 minutes

Cooking Time: 14 minutes

Servings: 3

Ingredients:

- 2 (8-ounce) rib eye steaks
- 2 tablespoons butter, melted
- Salt and ground black pepper, as required

Direction:

1. Coat the steak with butter and then, sprinkle with salt and black pepper evenly.
2. Press the "Power Button" of Ninja Foodi Digital Air Fry Oven and turn the dial to select the "Air Roast" mode.
3. Press the Time button and again turn the dial to set the cooking time to 14 minutes.
4. Now push the Temp button and rotate the dial to set the temperature at 400 degrees F.
5. Press the "Start /Pause" button to start.
6. When the unit beeps to show that it is preheated, open the lid and grease "Air Fry Basket".
7. Arrange the steaks into "Air Fry Basket" and insert them in the oven.

8. Remove from the oven and place steaks onto a platter for about 5 minutes.
9. Cut each steak into desired size slices and serve.

Nutrition: Calories 388, Total Fat 23.7 g, Saturated Fat 110.2 g, Cholesterol 154 mg, Sodium 278 mg, Total Carbs 0 g, Fiber 0 g, Sugar 0 g, Protein 41 g

Lamb

Middle Eastern Lamb Stew

Preparation Time: 10 minutes

Cooking Time: 20 minutes

Servings: 4

Ingredients:

- 2 tablespoons olive oil
- 1½ lb. lamb stew meat, sliced into cubes
- 1 onion, diced
- 6 garlic cloves, chopped
- 1 teaspoon cumin
- 1 teaspoon coriander
- 1 teaspoon turmeric
- 1 teaspoon cinnamon
- Salt and pepper to taste
- 2 tablespoons tomato paste
- ¼ cup red wine vinegar
- 2 tablespoons honey
- 1¼ cups chicken broth
- 15 oz. chickpeas, rinsed and drained
- ¼ cup raisins

Directions:

1. Choose Sauté on the Ninja Foodi. Add the oil. Cook the onion for 3 minutes.
2. Add the lamb and seasonings. Cook for 5 minutes, stirring frequently.
3. Stir in the rest of the ingredients. Cover the pot. Set it to Pressure.
4. Cook on high pressure for 50 minutes. Release the pressure naturally.

Nutrition: Calories: 867, Total Fat: 26.6 g, Saturated Fat: 6.3 g, Cholesterol: 153 mg, Sodium: 406 mg, Total Carbohydrate: 87.4 g, Dietary Fiber: 20.4 g, Total Sugars: 27.9 g, Protein: 71.2 g, Potassium: 1815 mg

Chorizo Cashew Soup

Preparation Time: 30-35 Minutes
Cooking Time: 70 Minutes

Servings: 5-6

Ingredients:
- 2 shallots, sliced
- 3 cloves garlic, minced
- 3 chorizo sausage, chopped
- 28 ounces fire-roasted diced tomatoes
- ½ cup ripe tomatoes
- 1 tablespoon red wine vinegar
- ½ cup thinly sliced fresh basil
- 4 cups beef broth
- ½ cup raw cashews
- 1 tablespoon olive oil
- 1 teaspoon salt
- ½ teaspoon ground black pepper

Directions:
1. Take your Ninja Foodi and place it over a dry kitchen platform. Plug it in and open the lid.
2. Pour the oil into the pot. Press "SEAR /SAUTÉ" cooking function. Adjust temperature level to "MD: HI".
3. Press the "START /STOP" button to start the cooking process. It will take 3-5 minutes to pre-heat.
4. When the oil is simmering, add the chorizo; stir and cook until crisp. Remove and transfer to a plate lined with a paper towel.
5. Add the garlic and onions; stir and cook to soften and turn translucent for 4-5 minutes. Season with salt.
6. Stir in the wine vinegar, broth, diced tomatoes, cashews, tomatoes, and black pepper.
7. Close the top by placing the pressing lid. Do not forget to set the pressure valve to a locked position.
8. Press the "PRESSURE" cooking function. Adjust the temperature level to "HI".
9. Adjust cooking time to 8 minutes. Press the "START /STOP" button to start the cooking process.
10. After cooking time is over, set the pressure valve to VENT position to release the build-up pressure quicker.
11. Add the mixture to a blender; blend to make a smooth soup.
12. Divide into serving plates or bowls; serve warm top with some basil and crisped chorizo.

Nutrition: Calories 347, Fat 22g, Carbohydrates 17g, Fiber 4g, Protein 14g

Bacon Potato Salad

Preparation Time: 20Minutes
Cooking Time: 70 Minutes

Servings: 5-6

Ingredients:
- 6 slices smoked bacon, chopped
- 2 red onions, sliced
- 6 red potatoes, peeled and quartered
- ½ cup of water
- 1 teaspoon flat-leaf parsley, chopped
- 2 teaspoons mustard
- ½ cup apple cider vinegar
- 3 tablespoons honey
- 1 teaspoon salt
- 1 /3 teaspoon black pepper

Directions:
1. Take your Ninja Foodi and place it over a dry kitchen platform. Plug it in and open the lid.
2. Press "SEAR /SAUTÉ" cooking function. Adjust temperature level to "MD: HI".
3. Press the "START /STOP" button to start the cooking process. It will take 3-5 minutes to pre-heat.
4. In the pot, add the bacon and cook until crispy on both sides for 3-4 minutes. Set aside.

5. In a mixing bowl (medium-large size), combine honey, salt, mustard, vinegar, water, and black pepper.
6. In the pot, combine the potatoes, chopped bacon, honey mixture, and onions; stir the mixture.
7. Close the top by placing the pressing lid. Do not forget to set the temperature valve in a locked or sealed position.
8. Press the "PRESSURE" cooking function. Adjust and set pressure level to "HI".
9. Adjust cooking time to 6 minutes. Press the "START /STOP" button to start the cooking process.
10. After cooking time is over, allow the build-up pressure to get released for around 10 minutes in a natural manner. Then, set the pressure valve to VENT position in order to release the remaining pressure quicker.
11. Divide into serving plates or bowls; serve warm with some parsley on top.

Nutrition: Calories 413, Fat 17g, Carbohydrates 47g, Fiber 4g, Protein 13g

Lamb Curry

Preparation Time: 10 minutes

Cooking Time: 10minutes

Servings: 4

Ingredients:

- 1½ lb. lamb stew meat, cubed
- 1 tablespoon lime juice
- 4 cloves garlic, minced
- ½ cup of coconut milk
- 1-inch piece fresh ginger, grated
- Salt and pepper to taste
- 1 tablespoon coconut oil
- 14 oz. diced tomatoes
- ¾ teaspoon turmeric
- 1 tablespoon curry powder
- 1 onion, diced

- 3 carrots, sliced

Directions:

1. In a bowl, toss the lamb meat in lime juice, garlic, coconut milk, ginger, salt, and pepper. Marinate for 30 minutes.
2. Put the meat with its marinade and the rest of the ingredients into the Ninja Foodi.
3. Mix well. Seal the pot. Set it to Pressure. Cook at high pressure for 20 minutes.
4. Release the pressure naturally.

Nutrition: Calories: 631, Total Fat: 31.4 g, Saturated Fat: 18.4 g, Cholesterol: 204 mg, Sodium: 230 mg, Total Carbohydrate: 19.7 g, Dietary Fiber: 5.7 g, Total Sugars: 9.5 g, Protein: 67.2 g, Potassium: 1490 mg

Filet Mignon with Pineapple Salsa

Preparation Time: 15 Minutes

Cooking Time: 8 Minutes

Servings: 4

Ingredients:

- 4 (6- to 8-ounce) filet mignon steaks
- 1 tablespoon canola oil, divided
- Sea salt
- Freshly ground black pepper
- ½ medium pineapple, cored and diced
- 1 medium red onion, diced
- 1 jalapeño pepper, seeded, stemmed, and diced
- 1 tablespoon freshly squeezed lime juice
- ¼ cup chopped fresh cilantro leaves
- Chili powder
- Ground coriander

Directions:

1. Rub each filet on all sides with ½ tablespoon of the oil, then season with the salt and pepper.

2. Insert the Grill Grate and close the hood. Select GRILL, set temperature to HIGH, and set time to 8 minutes. Select START /STOP to begin preheating.
3. When the unit beeps to signify it has preheated, add the filets to the Grill Grate. Gently press the filets down to maximize grill marks, then close the hood.
4. After 4 minutes, open the hood and flip the filets. Close the hood and continue cooking for an additional 4 minutes, or until the filets' internal temperature reads 125°F on a food thermometer. Remove the filets from the grill; they will continue to cook (called carry-over cooking) to a food-safe temperature even after you've removed them from the grill.
5. Let the filets rest for a total of 10 minutes; this allows the natural juices to redistribute into the steak.

Nutrition: Calories: 571; Total fat: 25g; Saturated fat: 8g; Cholesterol: 192mg; Sodium: 264mg; Carbohydrates: 20g; Fiber: 3g; Protein: 65g

Gochujang-Marinated Baby Back Ribs

Preparation Time: 10 Minutes

Cooking Time: 22 Minutes

Servings: 4

Ingredients:

- ¼ cup gochujang paste
- ¼ cup soy sauce
- ¼ cup freshly squeezed orange juice
- 2 tablespoons apple cider vinegar
- 2 tablespoons sesame oil
- 6 garlic cloves, minced
- 1½ tablespoons brown sugar
- 1 tablespoon grated fresh ginger
- 1 teaspoon salt

- 4 (8- to 10-ounce) baby back ribs

Directions:

1. In a medium bowl, add the gochujang paste, soy sauce, orange juice, vinegar, oil, garlic, sugar, ginger, and salt, and stir to combine.
2. Place the baby back ribs on a baking sheet and coat all sides with the sauce. Cover with aluminum foil and refrigerate for 6 hours.
3. Insert the Grill Grate and close the hood. Select GRILL, set the temperature to MEDIUM, and set the time to 22 minutes. Select START /STOP to begin preheating.
4. When the unit beeps to signify it has preheated, place the ribs on the Grill Grate. Close the hood and cook for 11 minutes. After 11 minutes, flip the ribs, close the hood, and cook for an additional 11 minutes.

Nutrition: Calories: 826; Total fat: 64g; Saturated fat: 22g; Cholesterol: 191mg; Sodium: 2113mg; Carbohydrates: 19g; Fiber: 1g; Protein: 41g

Glazed Lamb Chops

Preparation Time: 10 minutes

Cooking Time: 15 minutes

Servings: 4

Ingredients:

- 1 tablespoon Dijon mustard
- ½ tablespoon fresh lime juice
- 1 teaspoon honey
- ½ teaspoon olive oil
- Salt and ground black pepper, as required
- 4 (4-ounce) lamb loin chops

Direction:

1. In a black pepper large bowl, mix the mustard, lemon juice, oil, honey, salt, and black pepper.
2. Add the chops and coat with the mixture generously.
3. Place the chops onto the greased "Sheet Pan".
4. Press the "Power Button" of Ninja Foodi Digital Air Fry Oven and turn the dial to select the "Air Bake" mode.
5. Press the Time button and again turn the dial to set the cooking time to 15 minutes.
6. Now push the Temp button and rotate the dial to set the temperature at 390 degrees F.
7. Press the "Start /Pause" button to start.
8. When the unit beeps to show that it is preheated, open the lid.
9. Insert the "Sheet Pan" in the oven.
10. Flip the chops once halfway through.
11. Serve hot.

Nutrition: Calories 224, Total Fat 9.1 g, Saturated Fat 3.1 g, Cholesterol 102 mg, Sodium 169 mg, Total Carbs 1.7 g, Fiber 0.1 g, Sugar 1.5 g, Protein 32 g

Buttered Leg of Lamb

Preparation Time: 15 minutes

Cooking Time: 1¼ hours

Servings: 8

Ingredients:

- (2¼-pound) boneless leg of lamb
- tablespoons butter, melted
- Salt and ground black pepper, as required
- fresh rosemary sprigs

Direction:

1. Rub the leg of lamb with butter and sprinkle with salt and black pepper.

2. Wrap the leg of lamb with rosemary sprigs.
3. Press the "Power Button" of Ninja Foodi Digital Air Fry Oven and turn the dial to select the "Air Fry" mode.
4. Press the Time button and again turn the dial to set the cooking time to 75 minutes.
5. Now push the Temp button and rotate the dial to set the temperature at 300 degrees F.
6. Press the "Start /Pause" button to start.
7. When the unit beeps to show that it is preheated, open the lid and grease "Air Fry Basket".
8. Arrange the leg of lamb into "Air Fry Basket" and insert it in the oven.
9. Remove from oven and place the leg of lamb onto a cutting board for about 10 minutes before slicing.
10. Cut into desired sized pieces and serve.

Nutrition: Calories 278, Total Fat 13.8 g, Saturated Fat 6.1 g, Cholesterol 126 mg, Sodium 147 mg, Total Carbs 0.5 g, Fiber 0.4 g, Sugar 0 g, Protein 35.9 g

Herbed Lamb Chops

Preparation Time: 5-10 Minutes

Cooking Time: 13 Minutes

Servings: 6

Ingredients:

- 3 pounds lamb chops
- 3 tablespoons olive oil
- 3 basil leaves, crushed
- 2 teaspoons dried oregano, crushed
- Salt and ground black pepper to taste
- 1 clove garlic, minced
- 1 bay leaf
- 1 fresh rosemary spring
- 1 cup chicken broth

Directions:

1. In a mixing bowl, mix the oregano, salt, and black pepper. Rub the lamb chops with the herb mixture.
2. Take Ninja Foodi multi-cooker, arrange it over a cooking platform, and open the top lid.
3. In the pot, add the butter; Select "SEAR /SAUTÉ" mode and select "MD: HI" pressure level.
4. Press "STOP /START." After about 4-5 minutes, the butter will melt.
5. Add the basil, rosemary, garlic, and bay leaf and cook for about 1 minute. Add the lamb chops and cook for about 4 minutes per side.
6. Seal the multi-cooker by locking it with the pressure lid; ensure to keep the pressure release valve locked /sealed.
7. Select "PRESSURE" mode and select the "HI" pressure level. Then, set the timer to 5 minutes and press "STOP /START"; it will start the cooking process by building up inside pressure.
8. When the timer goes off, quick release pressure by adjusting the pressure valve to the VENT. After pressure gets released, open the pressure lid. Serve warm.

Nutrition: Calories: 483, Fat: 24.5g, Saturated Fat: 3g, Trans Fat: 0g, Carbohydrates: 2g, Fiber: 0.5g, Sodium: 328mg, Protein: 11g

Simple Lamb Chop

Preparation Time: 5 minutes

Cooking Time 25 minutes

Servings: 2

Ingredients:

- 2 medium lamb chops
- 1 tbsp. lemon juice
- 1 tsp dried rosemary
- 1 tsp dried thyme
- Salt and pepper to taste

Directions:

1. Preheat the Ninja Air Fryer to 350 degrees F.
2. Combine all the ingredients to season the lamb chops thoroughly.
3. Place the lamb chops in the air fryer basket for 25 minutes.
4. Allow the lamb chops to rest for 10 minutes before serving.

Nutrition: Calories: 265 kcal, Carbs: 5.9 g, Fat: 15.2 g, Protein: 25.2 g.

Herbed Rack of Lamb

Preparation Time: 7 minutes

Cooking Time 10 minutes

Servings: 4

Ingredients:

- 1 rack of lamb
- 3 tbsp. olive oil
- 1 tbsp. dried rosemary
- 1 tbsp. dried thyme
- 2 garlic cloves, minced
- Salt and pepper to taste

Directions:

1. Preheat the ninja air fryer to 360 degrees F.
2. Combine all the ingredients except the rack of lamb in a small bowl to form the seasoning.
3. Rub the mixture all over the rack of lamb and place the rack of lamb into the air fryer basket. Cook for 10-minutes and check the internal temperature. For rare meat, the internal temperature should be 145 degrees F. For medium meat, the internal temperature should be 160 degrees F. For well-done meat, the internal temperature should be 170 degrees F.

4. Serve with your favorite sides after the lamb has rested for a minimum of 10 minutes.

Nutrition: Calories: 287 kcal, Carbs: 1.5 g, Fat: 20.7 g, Protein: 23.2 g.

Leg of Lamb

Preparation Time: 5 minutes

Cooking Time 40 minutes

Servings: 5

Ingredients:

- 1 leg of lamb
- Salt and pepper to taste

Directions:

1. Preheat the ninja air fryer to 360 degrees F.
2. Season the leg of lamb with salt and pepper then place in the air fryer basket. Cook for 40 minutes.
3. Serve warm with desired sides

Nutrition: Calories: 243 kcal, Carbs: 0 g, Fat: 9.6 g, Protein: 36. g.

Lamb Chops in Tomato Sauce

Preparation Time: 10 minutes

Cooking Time: 10 hours

Servings: 6

Ingredients:

- 1 pound lamb chops
- 1½ cups tomatoes, chopped finely
- 1 cup chicken broth
- Salt and ground black pepper, as required
- 3 tablespoon mixed fresh herbs (oregano, thyme, sage), chopped

Directions:

1. In the pot of Ninja Foodi, place all the ingredients and mix well.
2. Close the Ninja Foodi with a crisping lid and select "Slow Cooker".
3. Set on "Low" for 8 hours.
4. Press "Start/Stop" to begin cooking.
5. Open the lid and serve hot.

Nutrition: Calories: 371, Fat: 19.1 g, Saturated Fat: 6.2 g, Carbohydrates: 4.5 g, Fiber 1.2 g, Sodium 255 mg, Protein: 45.4 g

Braised Leg of Lamb

Preparation Time: 15 minutes

Cooking Time: 37 minutes

Servings: 10

Ingredients:

- 1 (4-pound) bone-in leg of lamb
- Salt and ground black pepper, as required
- 1 tablespoon olive oil
- 1 large yellow onion, sliced thinly
- 1½ cups chicken broth, divided
- 2 tablespoons fresh lemon juice
- 6 garlic cloves, crushed
- 6 fresh thyme sprigs
- 3 fresh rosemary sprigs

Directions:

1. Season the leg of lamb with salt and black pepper generously
2. Select the "Sauté/Sear" setting of Ninja Foodi and place the butter into the pot.
3. Press "Start/Stop" to begin cooking and heat for about 2-3 minutes.
4. Add the leg of lamb and sear for about 4 minutes per side.
5. Transfer the leg of the lamb onto a large plate.
6. In the pot, add the onion and a little salt and cook for about 3 minutes.

7   Add a little broth and cook for about 2 minutes, scraping the brown bits from the bottom.
8   Press "Start/Stop" to stop cooking and stir in the cooked leg of lamb and remaining ingredients.
9   Close the Ninja Foodi with the pressure lid and place the pressure valve in the "Seal" position.
10 Select "Pressure" and set it to "High" for 75 minutes.
11 Press "Start/Stop" to begin cooking.
12 Do a "Natural" release.
13 Open the lid and with tongs, transfer the leg of lamb onto a cutting board for about 10 minutes.
14 Strain the pan liquid into a bowl.
15 Cut the leg of lamb into desired sized slices.
16 Pour strained liquid over the sliced leg of lamb and serve.

Nutrition: Calories: 626, Fat: 42.3, Saturated Fat: 19.5 g, Carbohydrates: 2.6 g, Fiber 0.6 g, Sodium 303 mg, Protein: 54.4 g

Lamb Meatballs in Mushroom Sauce

Preparation Time: 15 minutes

Cooking Time: 22 minutes

Servings: 6

Ingredients:

- 1½ pounds ground lamb
- 2 tablespoons dried onion, minced
- ¼ cup fresh parsley, minced
- 2 teaspoons dried sage
- ½ teaspoon fennel seeds, crushed
- ½ teaspoon ground nutmeg
- ½ teaspoon garlic powder
- Salt and ground black pepper, as required
- 8 ounces fresh button mushrooms, sliced
- 1 large onion, chopped
- ¼ cup beef broth

- ¼ cup low-sodium soy sauce
- 2 tablespoons cornstarch
- ½ cup unsweetened coconut milk

Directions:

1. In a large bowl, add the lamb, dried onion, parsley, sage, fennel seeds, nutmeg, garlic powder, salt, and black pepper and mix until well combined.
2. Make 1-inch meatballs from the mixture.
3. In the pot of Ninja Foodi, place the mushrooms, onion, broth, and soy sauce and stir to combine.
4. Arrange the meatballs on top of the mushroom mixture.
5. Close the Ninja Foodi with the pressure lid and place the pressure valve in the "Seal" position.
6. Select "Pressure" and set it to "High" for 20 minutes.
7. Press "Start/Stop" to begin cooking.
8. Switch the valve to "Vent" and do a "Quick" release.
9. Meanwhile, in a small bowl, add the cornstarch and coconut milk and mix well.
10. Open the lid and select the "Sauté/Sear" setting of Ninja Foodi.
11. Stir in the cornstarch mixture cook for about 1-2 minutes.
12. Press "Start/Stop" to stop cooking and serve hot.

Nutrition: Calories: 285, Fat: 13.4 g, Saturated Fat: 7.3 g, Carbohydrates: 6.5 g, Fiber 1.2 g, Sodium 739 mg, Protein: 34.6 g

Crazy Greek Lamb Gyros

Preparation time: 10 minutes

Cooking time: 25 minutes

Servings: 8

Ingredients:

- 8 garlic cloves

- 1 and ½ teaspoon salt
- 2 teaspoons dried oregano
- 1 and ½ cups of water
- 2 pounds lamb meat, ground
- 2 teaspoons rosemary
- ½ teaspoon pepper
- 1 small onion, chopped
- 2 teaspoons ground marjoram

Directions:

1. Add onions, garlic, marjoram, rosemary, salt, and pepper to a food processor
2. Process until combined well, add round lamb meat, and process again
3. Press meat mixture gently into a loaf pan
4. Transfer the pan to your Ninja Foodi pot
5. Lock lid and select "Bake/Roast" mode
6. Bake for 25 minutes at 375 degrees F
7. Transfer to serving dish and enjoy!

Nutrition: Calories: 242, Fat: 15g, Carbohydrates: 2.4g, Protein: 21g

Every day Lamb Roast

Preparation time: 10 minutes

Cooking time: 60 minutes

Servings: 6

Ingredients:

- 2 pounds lamb roasted Wegmans
- 1 cup onion soup
- 1 cup beef broth
- Salt and pepper to taste

Directions:

1. Transfer lamb roast to your Ninja Foodi pot
2. Add onion soup, beef broth, salt, and pepper
3. Lock lid and cook on Medium-HIGH pressure for 55 minutes
4. Release pressure naturally over 10 minutes
5. Transfer to a serving bowl, serve, and enjoy!

Nutrition: Calories: 349, Fat: 18g, Carbohydrates: 2.9g, Protein: 39g

Fish and Seafood

Cedar-Plank Salmon

Preparation Time: 30 Minutes

Cooking Time: 2 Hours and 30 Minutes

Servings: 6

Ingredients:

- 2 - Tbsp grainy mustard
- 2 - Tbsp mild honey or pure maple syrup
- 1 - teaspoon Minced rosemary
- 1 - Tbsp grated lemon zest
- 1 (2-pounds) salmon fillet with skin (1½ inches thick)

Directions:

1. Splash cedar Ninja oven broiling board in water to cover 2 HRS, keeping it inundated.
2. Plan barbecue for direct-heat cooking over medium-hot charcoal. Open vents on the base and top of a charcoal Ninja oven broil.
3. Mix mustard, nectar, rosemary, pizzazz, and½ teaspoon every one of salt and pepper. Spread blends on the substance side of salmon and let remain at room temperature 15MIN.
4. Put salmon on board, skin side down. Barbecue, secured with a cover, until salmon is simply cooked through and edges are seared, 13 to 15MIN. Let salmon remain on board 5MIN before serving.

Nutrition: Calories 240, Fat 15g, Carbohydrate 0g, Protein 23g.

Grilled Coconut Shrimp with Shishito Peppers

Preparation Time: 25 Minutes

Cooking Time: 25 Minutes

Servings: 4

Ingredients:

- 6 - garlic cloves, finely grated
- - Tbsp. finely grated lime zest
- ¼ cup low sodium
- ¼ cup grapeseed or vegetable oil
- 1 lb. large shrimp, peeled, deveined
- ½ cup toasted unsweetened shredded coconut
- 8 - oz. shish to peppers
- ½ cup basil leaves
- ¼ cup fresh lime juice
- Flaky sea salt

Directions:

1. Mix garlic, lime get-up-and-go, soy sauce, and ¼ cup oil in a medium bowl. Add shrimp and hurl to cover. Include ½ cup coconut and hurl again to cover. Let sit while the Ninja oven broil warms, in any event, 5MIN and up to 30MIN.
2. Set up a Ninja oven broil for high warmth, delicately oil grind.
3. Cautiously organize shrimp in an even layer on the mesh. Ninja oven broil, cautiously turning part of the way through, until hazy and daintily singed, about 2MIN. A portion of the coconuts will tumble off all the while, and that is alright. Move to a serving platter.
4. Ninja oven broil peppers, turning every so often and being mindful so as not to let them fall through the mesh until delicately roasted all over about 6MIN. Move to platter with shrimp.
5. Top shrimp and peppers with basil, shower with a lime squeeze, and sprinkle with ocean salt and more coconut.

Nutrition: Calories 82, Fat 7g, Carbohydrate 4g, Protein 2g.

Clams with Spicy Tomato Broth and Garlic Mayo

Preparation Time: 10 Minutes

Cooking Time: 50 Minutes

Servings: 4

Ingredients:

- ½ lemon
- 5 - garlic cloves, 1 whole, 4 thinly sliced
- ½ cup mayonnaise
- Kosher salt
- ¼ cup plus 3 Tbsp. extra-virgin olive oil
- 2 - large shallots, thinly sliced
- - red Chile (such as Holland or Fresno), thinly sliced, or½ tsp. crushed red pepper flakes
- - Tbsp. tomato paste
- - cups cherry tomatoes
- 1 - cup dry white wine
- 36 - littleneck clams, scrubbed
- 6 - Tbsp. unsalted butter, cut into pieces
- - Tbsp. finely chopped chives
- - thick slices of country-style bread

Directions:

1. Set up a Ninja Foodi oven broil for medium warmth. Finely grind the get-up-and-go from lemon half into a little bowl, at that point crush in the juice. Finely grind the entire garlic clove into a bowl and blend in mayonnaise. Season garlic mayo with salt and put it in a safe spot.
2. Spot a huge cast-iron skillet on the Ninja Foodi oven broil and warmth ¼ cup oil in a skillet. Include cut garlic, shallots, and Chile and cook, mixing regularly, until simply mollified, about 2MIN. Include tomato glue and cook, mixing frequently, until glue obscures somewhat, around 1 MIN. Include tomatoes and a touch of salt and cook, mixing every so often, until tomatoes mellow and discharge their juices, about 4MIN. Include wine and cook until it is nearly decreased considerably and no longer scents boozy about 3MIN.

3. Add shellfishes and margarine to the skillet and spread. Cook until shellfishes have opened, 6–10MIN, contingent upon the size of mollusks and warmth level. Expel skillet from Ninja Foodi oven broil; dispose of any mollusks that do not open. Sprinkle with chives.
4. In the interim, shower bread with the staying 3 Tbsp. oil and season softly with salt. Barbecue until brilliant earthy colored and fresh, about 3MIN per side.
5. Serve mollusks with toasted bread and saved garlic mayo.

Nutrition: Calories 282, Fat 10g, Carbohydrate 0g, Protein 20g.

Grilled Swordfish with Tomatoes and Oregano

Preparation Time: 10 Minutes

Cooking Time: 40 Minutes

Servings: 4

Ingredients:

- ½ cup plus 2 Tbsp. extra-virgin olive oil, plus more for the grill
- 2 - Tbsp. pine nuts
- 2 - (12-oz.) swordfish steaks, about 1" thick
- Kosher salt, freshly ground pepper
- ¼ cup red wine vinegar
- 2 - Tbsp. drained capers, finely chopped
- - Tbsp. finely chopped oregano, plus 2 sprigs for serving
- ½ tsp. honey
- - large ripe heirloom tomatoes, halved, thickly sliced

Directions:

1. Set up a Ninja Foodi oven broil for medium-high warmth; delicately oil

grind. Toast pine nuts in a dry little skillet over medium warmth, shaking frequently, until brilliant, about 4MIN. Let cool and put in a safe spot for serving.
2. Pat swordfish dry and season did with salt and pepper. Spot on a rimmed preparing sheet and let sit at room temperature 15MIN.
3. Then, whisk vinegar, tricks, hacked oregano, nectar, and½ cup oil in a little bowl to consolidate; put the marinade in a safe spot. Mastermind tomatoes on a rimmed platter, covering somewhat; put in a safe spot.
4. Rub swordfish done with the staying 2 Tbsp. oil and Ninja Foodi oven broil, undisturbed, until barbecue marks show up, about 4MIN. cautiously turn over and cook on the second side until fish is misty entirely through, about 4MIN. Move to saved platter with tomatoes and top with oregano branches. Season with increasingly salt and pepper. Pour held marinade over and let sit in any event 15MIN and if 60 minutes. To serve, disperse saved pine nuts over.

Nutrition: Calories 210, Fat 10g, Carbohydrate 0g, Protein 30g.

Grilled Spiced Snapper with Mango and Red Onion Salad

Preparation Time: 10 Minutes

Cooking Time: 30 Minutes

Servings: 4

Ingredients:

- (5-lb.) or 2 (2½-lb.) head-on whole fish, cleaned
- Kosher salt
- 1 /3 - cup chat masala, vadouvan, or tandoori spice

- 1 /3 - cup vegetable oil, plus more for the grill
- 1 - ripe but firm mango, peeled, cut into irregular 1½" pieces
- 1 - small red onion, thinly sliced, rinsed
- 1 - bunch cilantro, coarsely chopped
- - Tbsp. fresh lime juice
- Extra-virgin olive oil
- Lime wedges (for serving)

Directions:

1. Spot fish on a cutting board and pat dry altogether with paper towels. With a sharp blade, make slices across on an askew along the body each 2" on the two sides, chopping right down to the bones. Season fish liberally all around with salt. Coat fish with flavor blend, pressing on more if necessary. Let sit at room temperature 20MIN.
2. In the interim, set up a Ninja Foodi oven broil for medium-high warmth. Clean and oil grind.
3. Shower the two sides of fish with staying 1 /3 cup vegetable oil to cover. Ninja Foodi oven broils fish undisturbed, 10MIN. Lift up somewhat from one edge to check whether the skin is puffed and softly roasted and effectively discharges from the mesh. If not exactly prepared, take off alone for another MIN or somewhere in the vicinity and attempt once more. When it is prepared, delicately slide 2 huge metal spatulas underneath and turn over. Barbecue fish until the opposite side is daintily roasted and skin is puffed, 8–12MIN, contingent upon the size of the fish. Move to a platter.
4. Sling mango, onion, cilantro, lime juice, and a major spot of salt in a medium bowl. Sprinkle with a touch of olive oil and sling again to cover. Disperse a mango plate of mixed greens over fish and present with lime wedges for pressing over.

Nutrition: Calories 224, Fat 9g, carbohydrate 17g, Protein 24g.

Grilled Shrimp, Zucchini, and Tomatoes with Feta

Preparation Time: 30 Minutes

Cooking Time: 2 Hours and 30 Minutes

Servings: 6

Ingredients:

- 1 - large garlic clove, finely grated
- 2 - Tsp finely chopped oregano
- ¾ teaspoon kosher salt
- ¼ teaspoon crushed red pepper flakes
- 2 - Tbsp olive oil, plus more for a grill basket
- 10 - jumbo shrimp (about 8 ounces), peeled, deveined, tails left on
- 1 - medium zucchini (about 8 ounces), sliced into ¼" rounds
- 1 - pint cherry tomatoes
- 2 - pita pockets
- 1 /3 - cup crumbled feta (about 1.5 ounces)
- Special Equipment
- A flat grill basket (about 13½ x 8½")

Directions:

1. Set up a Ninja Foodi oven broil for high warmth. Whisk garlic, oregano, salt, red pepper, and 2 Tbsp. oil in an enormous bowl. Include shrimp, zucchini, and tomatoes and hurl to cover.
2. Brush wires of Ninja Foodi oven broil container with oil, at that point, include shrimp blend. Mastermind in an even layer and close container. Spot barbecue container on Ninja Foodi oven broil and cook, turning regularly until shrimp are completely cooked through and zucchini and tomatoes are delicately singed about 6MIN.
3. In the meantime, barbecue pita just until warm and toasted.
4. Move shrimp blend to an enormous bowl and hurl until covered with

tomato juices. Partition among plates and top with feta. Present with pita close by.

Nutrition: Calories 178, Fat 3g, Carbohydrate 12g, Protein 24g.

Grilled Salmon Steaks with Cilantro-Garlic Yogurt Sauce

Preparation Time: 10 Minutes

Cooking Time: 30 Minutes

Servings: 4

Ingredients:

- Vegetable oil (for the grill)
- 2 - Serrano chiles
- 2 - garlic cloves
- - cup cilantro leaves with tender stems
- ½ - cup plain whole-milk Greek yogurt
- 1 - Tbsp. extra-virgin olive oil
- 1 - tsp. honey
- - (12-oz.) bone-in salmon steaks
- Kosher salt

Directions:

1. Set up a Ninja Foodi oven broil for medium-high warmth; oil grind. Expel and dispose of seeds from 1 Chile. Purée the two chiles, garlic, cilantro, yogurt, oil, nectar, and ¼ cup water in a blender until smooth, season well with salt. Move half of the sauce to a little bowl and put it in a safe spot for serving.
2. Season salmon steaks daintily with salt. Barbecue, turning on more than one occasion until the substance is beginning to turn misty, about 4MIN. Keep on Ninja Foodi oven broiling, turning regularly and seasoning with residual sauce, until misty completely through, about 4MIN longer. Present withheld sauce nearby.

Nutrition: Calories 282, Fat 15g, Carbohydrate 0g, Protein 34g.

Rosemary Garlic Salmon

Preparation Time: 5-10 Minutes

Cooking Time: 12 Minutes

Servings: 2

Ingredients:

- 1 /4 teaspoon pepper
- 1 garlic clove, minced
- 1 /4 teaspoon salt
- 1 /4 teaspoon minced fresh rosemary
- 1 teaspoon grated lemon zest
- 2 salmon fillets (6 ounces each)

Directions:

1. In a mixing bowl, add all the ingredients except the salmon. Combine the ingredients to mix well with each other. Add the salmon and combine it well. Set aside for 15 minutes to marinate.
2. Take Ninja Foodi Grill, arrange it over your kitchen platform, and open the top lid.
3. Arrange the grill grate and close the top lid.
4. Press "GRILL" and select the "MED" grill function. Adjust the timer to 6 minutes and then press "START /STOP." Ninja Foodi will start pre-heating.
5. Ninja Foodi is preheated and ready to cook when it starts to beep. After you hear a beep, open the top lid.
6. Arrange the salmon over the grill grate.
7. Close the top lid and cook for 3 minutes. Now open the top lid, flip the salmon.
8. Close the top lid and cook for 3 more minutes.
9. Serve warm.

Nutrition: Calories:253, Fat:7.5g, Saturated Fat:3g, Trans Fat:0g, Carbohydrates:22.5g, Fiber: 3g, Sodium: 374mg, Protein: 36.5g

Nutrition: Calories: 286, Fat: 11.5g, Saturated Fat: 3.5g, Trans Fat: 0g, Carbohydrates: 18.5g, Fiber: 2g, Sodium: 712mg, Protein: 29.5g

Shrimp Lettuce Salad

Preparation Time: 10 Minutes

Cooking Time: 5 Minutes

Servings: 4

Ingredients:

- 3 garlic cloves, minced
- Sea salt and ground black pepper to taste
- 1-pound jumbo shrimps
- Juice of ½ lemon
- 2 heads romaine lettuce, chopped
- ¾ cup Caesar dressing
- ½ cup grated Parmesan cheese

Directions:

1. In a mixing bowl, add the shrimps with lemon juice, garlic, salt, and black pepper. Combine the ingredients to mix well with each other.
2. Take Ninja Foodi Grill, arrange it over your kitchen platform, and open the top lid.
3. Arrange the grill grate and close the top lid.
4. Press "GRILL" and select the "MAX" grill function. Adjust the timer to 5 minutes and then press "START /STOP." Ninja Foodi will start pre-heating.
5. Ninja Foodi is preheated and ready to cook when it starts to beep. After you hear a beep, open the top lid.
6. Arrange the shrimps over the grill grate.
7. Close the top lid and allow it to cook until the timer reads zero. Combine the romaine lettuce with the Caesar dressing.
8. Serve the shrimps warm with the Caesar mixture and cheese on top.

Butter Spiced Grilled Salmon

Preparation Time: 5-10 Minutes

Cooking Time: 10 Minutes

Servings: 4

Ingredients:

- 2 teaspoons cayenne pepper
- 2 pounds salmon fillets
- 2 teaspoons salt
- 6 tablespoons butter, melted
- 1 ¼ teaspoon onion salt
- 2 tablespoons lemon pepper
- 1 teaspoon white pepper, ground
- 1 teaspoon black pepper, ground
- 3 tablespoons smoked paprika
- 1 teaspoon dry basil
- 1 teaspoon ancho chili powder
- 1 teaspoon dry oregano
- Lemon wedges and dill sprigs

Directions:

1. Season the salmon fillets with butter. In a mixing bowl, add other ingredients. Combine well.
2. Coat the salmon with the bowl mixture.
3. Take Ninja Foodi Grill, arrange it over your kitchen platform, and open the top lid.
4. Arrange the grill grate and close the top lid.
5. Press "GRILL" and select the "MED" grill function. Adjust the timer to 10 minutes and then press "START /STOP." Ninja Foodi will start preheating.
6. Ninja Foodi is preheated and ready to cook when it starts to beep. After you hear a beep, open the top lid.

7. Arrange the salmon fillets over the grill grate.
8. Close the top lid and cook for 5 minutes. Now open the top lid, flip the fillets.
9. Close the top lid and cook for 5 more minutes. Serve warm.

Nutrition: Calories: 362, Fat: 7.5g, Saturated Fat: 2g, Trans Fat: 0g, Carbohydrates: 17g, Fiber: 1g, Sodium: 342mg, Protein: 26.5g

Asparagus Salmon

Preparation Time: 5-10 Minutes

Cooking Time: 10 Minutes

Servings: 4

Ingredients:

- 4 tablespoons unsalted butter, melted
- ½ tablespoon maple (sugar-free) syrup
- 4 salmon fillets, frozen and skinless
- 1-pound asparagus
- 1 tablespoon olive oil
- Black pepper (ground) and salt to taste
- 2 garlic cloves, minced
- ½ teaspoon dried thyme
- 1 lemon, juiced
- ½ teaspoon dried rosemary

Directions:

1. In a mixing bowl, toss the asparagus, olive oil, salt, and black pepper. In another mixing bowl, combine the butter, maple syrup, salt, black pepper, lemon juice, rosemary, garlic, and thyme.
2. Take Ninja Foodi multi-cooker, arrange it over a cooking platform, and open the top lid. In the pot, add 1 cup of water and arrange the reversible rack. Place the salmon over it.
3. Seal the multi-cooker by locking it with the pressure lid; ensure to keep the pressure release valve locked /sealed.
4. Select the "PRESSURE" mode and select the "HI" pressure level. Then, set the timer to 2 minutes and press "STOP /START"; it will start the cooking process by building up inside pressure.
5. When the timer goes off, quick release pressure by adjusting the pressure valve to the VENT. After pressure gets released, open the pressure lid.
6. Brush the salmon with the herb mixture. Arrange the asparagus over.
7. Seal the multi-cooker by locking it with the crisping lid; ensure to keep the pressure release valve locked /sealed.
8. Select "BROIL" mode and select the "HI" pressure level. Then, set the timer to 7 minutes and press "STOP /START"; it will start the cooking process by building up inside pressure.
9. When the timer goes off, quick release pressure by adjusting the pressure valve to the VENT. After pressure gets released, open the pressure lid. Serve warm and enjoy!

Nutrition: Calories: 494, Fat: 24.5g, Saturated Fat: 5g, Trans Fat: 0g, Carbohydrates: 6g, Fiber: 2g, Sodium: 829mg, Protein: 42g

Zucchini Fish Patties

Preparation Time: 5-10 Minutes

Cooking Time: 15 Minutes

Servings: 5-6

Ingredients:

- 1 teaspoon baking soda
- 1 tablespoon lemon juice
- 1 teaspoon oregano
- 10 ounces mackerel, minced
- 1 medium zucchini, grated
- 1 tablespoon olive oil
- 2 garlic cloves, sliced
- ½ cup coconut flour
- 2 eggs
- 1 teaspoon red chili flakes

Directions:

1. Add the zucchini and fish to a bowl. Sprinkle the baking soda, lemon juice, oregano, and chili flakes. Mix in the garlic. In a mixing bowl, beat the eggs.
2. Add the whisked eggs to the fish mixture. Add the coconut flour and knead to make a smooth dough. Prepare patties from the mixture.
3. Take Ninja Foodi multi-cooker, arrange it over a cooking platform, and open the top lid.
4. In the pot, add some oil; Select "SEAR /SAUTÉ" mode and select "MD: HI" pressure level.
5. Press "STOP /START." After about 4-5 minutes, the oil will start simmering.
6. Add the patties and cook (while stirring) until it becomes evenly brown over both sides.
7. Serve the patties with low carb dip or fresh salad greens.

Nutrition: Calories: 246, Fat: 14.5g, Saturated Fat: 3g, Trans Fat: 0g, Carbohydrates: 7g, Fiber: 2.5g, Sodium: 479mg, Protein: 16g

Crispy Crab Patties

Preparation Time: 5-10 Minutes

Cooking Time: 10 Minutes

Servings: 4

Ingredients:

- 1 shallot, minced
- ¼ cup mayonnaise low carb
- About 12 ounces lump crabmeat
- ¼ cup minced parsley
- 2 tablespoons Dijon mustard
- 2 tablespoons almond flour
- Zest of 1 lemon
- 1 egg, beaten
- Ground black pepper and salt to taste

Directions:

1. In a mixing bowl, add all the ingredients. Combine the ingredients to mix well with each other. Prepare 4 patties from the mixture.
2. Take Ninja Foodi multi-cooker, arrange it over a cooking platform, and open the top lid.
3. In the pot, arrange a reversible rack and place the Crisping Basket over the rack.
4. In the basket, add the patties.
5. Seal the multi-cooker by locking it with the crisping lid; ensure to keep the pressure release valve locked /sealed.
6. Select the "AIR CRISP" mode and adjust the 375°F temperature level. Then, set the timer to 10 minutes and press "STOP /START"; it will start the cooking process by building up inside pressure. Flip the patties after 5 minutes.
7. When the timer goes off, quick release pressure by adjusting the pressure valve to the VENT.
8. After pressure gets released, open the pressure lid. Serve warm and enjoy!

Nutrition: Calories: 177, Fat: 13g, Saturated Fat: 2g. Trans Fat: 0g, Carbohydrates: 2.5g, Fiber: 0 Sodium: 358mg, Protein: 11g

Broccoli Cod

Preparation Time: 5-10 Minutes

Cooking Time: 16 Minutes

Servings: 4

Ingredients:

- 1 red bell pepper, deseeded and chopped
- 1 green bell pepper, deseeded and chopped
- 1 tablespoon olive oil
- 1 large head of broccoli, cut into little florets
- 1 cup pork rinds

- 4 tablespoons unsalted butter, melted
- 1 green chili, minced
- 1 cup chicken broth
- 1 teaspoon zest and juiced
- Black pepper (ground) and salt to taste
- ¼ cup chopped parsley
- 1 lemon
- 4 cod fillets

Directions:

1. Take a Ninja multi-cooker, arrange it over a cooking platform, and open the top lid.
2. In the pot, add the oil; Select "SEAR /SAUTÉ" mode and select "MD: HI" pressure level. Press "STOP /START." After about 4-5 minutes, the oil will start simmering.
3. Add the broccoli, bell peppers, green chili, and cook (while stirring) until they become softened for 1 minute. Mix in the chicken broth.
4. Seal the multi-cooker by locking it with the pressure lid; ensure to keep the pressure release valve locked /sealed.
5. Select the "PRESSURE" mode and select the "HI" pressure level. Then, set the timer to 3 minutes and press "STOP /START"; it will start the cooking process by building up inside pressure. When the timer goes off, quick release pressure by adjusting the pressure valve to the VENT. After pressure gets released, open the pressure lid.
6. In a mixing bowl, add the pork rinds, butter, parsley, lemon zest, lemon juice, and salt. Combine the ingredients to mix well with each other.
7. Add the mixture on top of the fish fillets. Arrange a reversible rack in the pot; place the fillets over it. Seal the multi-cooker by locking it with the crisping lid; ensure to keep the pressure release valve locked /sealed.
8. Select the "AIR CRISP" mode and adjust the 350°F temperature level. Then, set the timer to 12 minutes and press "STOP /START"; it will start the cooking process by building up inside pressure.

9. When the timer goes off, quick release pressure by adjusting the pressure valve to the VENT. After pressure gets released, open the pressure lid. Serve warm and enjoy!

Nutrition: Calories: 453, Fat: 29.5g, Saturated Fat: 8.5g, Trans Fat: 0g, Carbohydrates: 16g, Fiber: 7g, Sodium: 743mg, Protein: 34g

Fish & Fries

Cooking Time: 16 Minutes

Preparation time: 30 minutes

Servings: 4

Ingredients:

- 1 lb. potatoes, sliced into strips
- 2 tablespoons olive oil
- Salt and pepper to taste
- 1 /4 cup all-purpose flour
- 1 egg
- 2 tablespoons water
- 2 /3 cup cornflakes, crushed
- 1 tablespoon Parmesan cheese, grated
- 1 lb. cod fillets

Directions:

1. Coat the potato strips with oil, salt, and pepper. Place in the Ninja Foodi basket.
2. Seal the crisping lid and set it to air crisp.
3. Cook at 400 degrees F for 10 minutes, stirring halfway through.
4. While waiting, combine the flour with salt and pepper in one bowl.
5. In another bowl, beat the egg and add water.
6. In the third bowl, mix the cornflakes and Parmesan.
7. Dip each fillet in the flour mixture. Then dip into the second and third bowls.

8. Place in the Ninja Foodi basket. Seal the lid and choose air crisp function.
9. Cook at 400 degrees for 10 minutes.

Nutrition: Calories 312, Total Fat 10.8g, Saturated Fat 2.4g, Cholesterol 101mg, Sodium 191mg, Total Carbohydrate 28.1g, Dietary Fiber 3.1g, Total Sugars 1.9g, Protein 26.7g, Potassium 493mg

Ranch Fish Fillet

Preparation time: 20 minutes

Cooking Time: 16 Minutes

Servings: 4

Ingredients:

- 3 /4 cup bread crumbs
- packet dry ranch dressing mix
- 1/2 tablespoons vegetable oil
- eggs, beaten
- fish fillets

Directions:

1. Combine the bread crumbs and ranch mix in a bowl. Pour in the oil.
2. Dip each fish fillet into the egg and cover with the crumb mixture.
3. Place in the Ninja Foodi basket. Seal the lid. Select air crisp function.
4. Cook at 360 degrees F for 12 minutes, flipping halfway through.

Nutrition: Calories 425, Total Fat 25.4g, Saturated Fat 5.7g, Cholesterol 113mg, Sodium 697mg, Total Carbohydrate 30.4g, Dietary Fiber 1.4g, Total Sugars 1.4g, Protein 18.8g, Potassium 360mg

Paprika Salmon

Preparation time: 15 minutes

Cooking Time: 16 Minutes

Servings: 2

Ingredients:

- 2 salmon fillets
- 2 teaspoons avocado oil
- 2 teaspoons paprika
- Salt and pepper to taste

Directions:

1. Coat the salmon with oil. Season with salt, pepper, and paprika.
2. Place in the Ninja Foodi basket. Set it to air crisp function.
3. Seal the crisping lid. Cook at 390 degrees for 7 minutes.

Nutrition: Calories 248, Total Fat 11.9g, Cholesterol 78mg, Sodium 79mg, Total Carbohydrate 1.5g, Dietary Fiber 1g, Total Sugars 0.2g, Protein 34.9g, Potassium 748mg

Fish & Chips with Herb Sauce

Preparation time: 50 minutes

Cooking Time: 16 Minutes

Servings: 4

Ingredients:

- 2 potatoes, sliced into strips
- Salt to taste
- 1/4 cup flour
- 1 egg
- 1 teaspoon Dijon mustard
- 1/4 cup seasoned panko bread crumbs
- 1 /2 teaspoons olive oil
- cod fish fillets

For the sauce:

- 1/4 cup light mayonnaise
- 2 tablespoons sour cream
- 2 tablespoons dill pickle, chopped
- 2 tablespoons red onion, chopped
- 1 tablespoon dill, chopped
- 1 tablespoon tarragon, chopped

- 2 teaspoons capers

Directions:

1. Soak the potato strips in a bowl of water for 30 minutes.
2. Drain the water and pat the potatoes dry using a paper towel.
3. Place the potato strips in the Ninja Foodi basket.
4. Seal the crisping lid and choose air crisp function.
5. Cook at 360 degrees for 25 minutes, turning once or twice.
6. Season with salt. Put the flour in a bowl.
7. Beat the egg and add the mustard to another bowl.
8. Mix the oil and bread crumbs on a shallow plate.
9. Coat the fish with the flour then the egg mixture, and then the oil with crumbs. Place in the basket. Cook at 360 degrees for 10 minutes.
10. Mix all the ingredients for the sauce and serve with the fish and fries.

Nutrition: Calories 409, Total Fat 12.1g, Saturated Fat 2.6g, Cholesterol 146mg, Sodium 426mg, Total Carbohydrate 27.9g, Dietary Fiber 3.2g, Total Sugars 2.6g, Protein 45.8g, Potassium 956mg

Southern Fried Fish Fillet

Preparation time: 30 minutes

Cooking Time: 16 Minutes

Servings: 4

Ingredients:

- 2 lb. white fish fillet
- 1 cup low-fat milk
- 1 lemon slice
- 1/2 cup mustard
- 1/2 cup cornmeal
- 1/4 cup all-purpose flour

- 2 tablespoons dried parsley flakes
- Salt and pepper to taste
- 1/4 teaspoon chili powder
- 1/4 teaspoon garlic powder
- 1/4 teaspoon onion powder
- 1/4 teaspoon cayenne pepper

Directions:

1. Place the fish fillet in a bowl. Pour the milk over the fish fillet.
2. Squeeze lemon slice over the fish. Marinate for 15 minutes.
3. Spread the mustard on the fish fillets.
4. In another bowl, mix the rest of the ingredients.
5. Coat the fish fillets with the cornmeal mixture. Place on the Ninja Foodi basket.
6. Set it to air crisp. Seal the crisping lid. Cook at 390 degrees for 10 minutes.
7. Flip the fillets and cook for 5 more minutes.

Nutrition: Calories 595, Total Fat 24g, Saturated Fat 3.4g, Cholesterol 178mg, Sodium 184mg, Total Carbohydrate 28.4g, Dietary Fiber 4.5g, Total Sugars 4.8g, Protein 64.7g, Potassium 1221mg

Fish Sticks

Preparation time: 20 minutes

Cooking Time: 16 Minutes

Servings: 2

Ingredients:

- 1 lb. cod, sliced into strips
- 1/2 cup tapioca starch
- 2 eggs
- 1 teaspoon dried dill
- Salt and pepper to taste
- 1 cup almond flour
- 1 teaspoon onion powder
- 1/2 teaspoon mustard powder
- 2 tablespoons avocado oil

Directions:

1. Pat the cod fillet strips dry using a paper towel.
2. Place the tapioca starch in a bowl.
3. In another bowl, beat the eggs.
4. In a larger bowl, mix the dill, salt, pepper, almond flour, onion powder, and mustard powder. Dip each strip in the first, second, and third bowls.
5. Coat the Ninja Foodi basket with avocado oil.
6. Place the fish strips inside. Cook at 390 degrees F for 5 minutes.

Nutrition: Calories 549, Total Fat 15g, Saturated Fat 2.6g, Cholesterol 288mg, Sodium 246mg, Total Carbohydrate 39.4g, Dietary Fiber 2.7g, Total Sugars 2.2g, Protein 61g, Potassium 695mg

Fish Fillet with Pesto Sauce

Preparation time: 20 minutes

Cooking Time: 16 Minutes

Servings: 3

Ingredients:

- 3 white fish fillets
- 1 tablespoon olive oil
- Salt and pepper to taste
- 2 cups fresh basil leaves
- 2 cloves garlic, crushed
- 2 tablespoons pine nuts
- 1 tablespoon Parmesan cheese, grated
- 1 cup olive oil

Directions:

1. Coat the fish fillets with 1 tablespoon of olive oil. Season with salt and pepper.
2. Place in the Ninja Foodi basket. Cook at 320 degrees for 8 minutes.
3. While waiting, mix the remaining ingredients in a food processor.

4. Pulse until smooth. Spread the pesto sauce on both sides of the fish before serving.

Nutrition: Calories 383, Total Fat 22.6g, Saturated Fat 4.1g, Cholesterol 125mg, Sodium 188mg, Total Carbohydrate 2.2g, Dietary Fiber 0.5g, Total Sugars 0.3g, Protein 42.1g, Potassium 715mg

Coconut Shrimp

Preparation time: 20 minutes

Cooking Time: 16 Minutes

Servings: 4

Ingredients:

- 1/2 cup all-purpose flour
- 1/2 teaspoons black pepper
- eggs
- 1/3 cup panko bread crumbs
- /3 cup unsweetened coconut flakes
- 12 oz. shrimp, peeled and deveined
- Cooking spray
- Salt and pepper to taste
- 1/4 cup honey
- 1/4 cup lime juice

Directions:

1. Mix the flour and black pepper in a bowl. In another bowl, beat the egg.
2. In the third bowl, mix the bread crumbs and coconut flakes.
3. Dip each of the shrimp in the first, second, and third bowls.
4. Place in the Ninja Foodi basket. Set it to air crisp. Cover the crisping lid.
5. Cook at 400 degrees F for 8 minutes, turn halfway through.
6. Season with salt and pepper.
7. Mix the remaining ingredients and serve with the shrimp.

Nutrition: Calories 293, Total Fat 4.4g, Saturated Fat 1.3g, Cholesterol 261mg, Sodium 306mg, Total Carbohydrate 37.8g, Dietary

Fiber 1.1g, Total Sugars 18.2g, Protein 25.1g, Potassium 229mg

Hot Prawns

Preparation time: 15 minutes

Cooking Time: 16 Minutes

Servings: 4

Ingredients:

- 1 teaspoon chili flakes
- 1 teaspoon chili powder
- Salt and pepper to taste
- 12 king prawns
- 2 tablespoons mayonnaise
- 1 tablespoon ketchup
- 1 tablespoon wine vinegar

Directions:

1. Combine all the spices in a bowl. Toss the prawns in the spice mixture.
2. Place the prawns in the Ninja Foodi basket. Seal the crisping lid.
3. Choose air crisp function. Cook at 360 degrees for 8 minutes.
4. While waiting, mix the mayo, ketchup, and vinegar. Serve with the prawns.

Nutrition: Calories 490, Total Fat 27.8g, Saturated Fat 11.4g, Cholesterol 3mg, Sodium 177mg, Total Carbohydrate 8.7g, Dietary Fiber 0.5g, Total Sugars 8.9g, Protein 0.3g, Potassium 29mg

Crispy Shrimp

Preparation time: 20 minutes

Cooking Time: 16 Minutes

Servings: 4

Ingredients:

- 1 lb. shrimp, peeled and deveined

- 2 eggs
- 1 /2 cup bread crumbs
- 1 /2 cup onion, diced
- 1 teaspoon ginger
- 1 teaspoon garlic powder
- Salt and pepper to taste

Directions:

1. In one bowl, beat the two eggs. In another bowl, put the rest of the ingredients.
2. Dip the shrimp first in the eggs and then in the spice mixture.
3. Place in the Ninja Foodi basket. Seal the crisping lid. Choose air crisp function.
4. Cook at 350 degrees for 10 minutes.

Nutrition: Calories 229, Total Fat 4.9g, Saturated Fat 1.4g, Cholesterol 321mg, Sodium 407mg, Total Carbohydrate 13.8g, Dietary Fiber 1.1g, Total Sugars 1.8g, Protein 30.7g, Potassium 283mg

Salt and Pepper Shrimp

Preparation time: 20 minutes

Cooking Time: 16 Minutes

Servings: 4

Ingredients:

- 2 teaspoons peppercorns
- 1 teaspoon salt
- 1 teaspoons sugar
- 1 lb. shrimp
- 3 tablespoons rice flour
- 2 tablespoons oil

Directions:

1. Set the Ninja Foodi to sauté. Roast the peppercorns for 1 minute. Let them cool.
2. Crush the peppercorns and add the salt and sugar.

3. Coat the shrimp with this mixture and then with flour.
4. Sprinkle oil on the Ninja Foodi basket. Place the shrimp on top.
5. Cook at 350 degrees for 10 minutes, flipping halfway through.

Nutrition: Calories 228, Total Fat 8.9g, Saturated Fat 1.5g, Cholesterol 239mg, Sodium 859mg, Total Carbohydrate 9.3g, Dietary Fiber 0.5g, Total Sugars 1g, Protein 26.4g, Potassium 211mg

Tuna Patties

Preparation time: 30 minutes

Cooking Time: 16 Minutes

Servings: 2

Ingredients:

- 2 cans of tuna flakes
- 2 tablespoon almond flour
- 1 teaspoon dried dill
- 1 tablespoon mayo
- 1/2 teaspoon onion powder
- 1 teaspoon garlic powder
- Salt and pepper to taste
- 1 tablespoon lemon juice

Directions:

1. Mix all the ingredients in a bowl. Form patties. Set the tuna patties on the Ninja Foodi basket. Seal the crisping lid. Set it to air crisp.
2. Cook at 400 degrees for 10 minutes. Flip and cook for 5 more minutes.

Nutrition: Calories 141, Total Fat 6.4g, Saturated Fat 0.7g, Cholesterol 17mg, Sodium 148mg, Total Carbohydrate 5.2g, Dietary Fiber 1g, Total Sugars 1.2g, Protein 17g, Potassium 48mg

Vegetarian and Vegan Recipes

Penne with Mushrooms and Gruyère

Preparation Time: 10 Minutes

Cooking Time: 30 Minutes

Servings: 4

Ingredients:

- 8 ounces penne pasta
- 1 (12–fluid ounce) can evaporate milk, divided
- 1¼ cups water or Roasted Vegetable Stock
- 1½ teaspoons kosher salt (or ¾ teaspoon fine salt)
- 1 large egg
- 1½ teaspoons cornstarch
- 8 ounces Gruyère cheese, shredded
- 1 recipe Sautéed Mushrooms
- 2 tablespoons chopped fresh parsley
- 3 tablespoons sour cream
- 1½ cups panko breadcrumbs
- 3 tablespoons melted unsalted butter
- 3 tablespoons grated Parmesan or similar cheese

Directions:

1. Pour the penne into the inner pot. Add 6 fluid ounces (¾ cup) of evaporated milk, water, and salt.
2. Lock the Pressure Lid into place, making sure the valve is set to Seal. Select Pressure and adjust the pressure to High and the Cooking Time to 4 minutes. Press Start.
3. While the pasta cooks, in a small bowl, thoroughly whisk the remaining 6 fluid ounces (¾ cup) of evaporated milk with the egg. In another small bowl, sprinkle the cornstarch over the Gruyère cheese and toss to coat.
4. After cooking, let the pressure release naturally for 3 minutes, then quick release any remaining pressure.

Carefully unlock and remove the Pressure Lid.

5. Add the milk-egg mixture and a large handful of the Gruyère cheese and stir to melt the cheese. Add the rest of the Gruyère cheese in 3 or 4 batches, stirring to melt after each addition. Stir in the mushrooms, parsley, and sour cream.

6. In a medium bowl, stir together the panko, melted butter, and Parmesan cheese. Sprinkle the panko over the pasta.

7. Close the Crisping Lid. Select Broil and adjust the time to 5 minutes. Press Start. When done, the topping should be brown and crisp; if not, broil for 1 to 2 minutes more. Serve immediately.

Nutrition: Calories: 804, Total fat: 39g, Saturated fat: 22g, Cholesterol: 169mg, Sodium: 1437mg, Carbohydrates: 74g, Fiber: 3g, Protein: 38g

Easy Eggplant Parmesan

Preparation Time: 15 Minutes

Cooking Time: 40 Minutes

Servings: 4

Ingredients:

- 1 large eggplant, cut into ¾-inch-thick rounds
- 2 teaspoons kosher salt (or 1 teaspoon fine salt)
- 3 tablespoons melted unsalted butter
- 1½ cups panko breadcrumbs
- 1 /3 cup grated Parmesan or similar cheese
- 2 cups Marinara Sauce
- 1 cup shredded mozzarella cheese

Directions:

1. Sprinkle the eggplant slices on both sides with the salt and place on a wire rack over a rimmed baking sheet to drain for 5 to 10 minutes.

2. While the eggplant drains, in a medium bowl, stir together the melted butter, panko, and Parmesan cheese. Set aside.

3. Rinse the eggplant slices and blot them dry. Place them in a single layer (as much as possible) in the inner pot and cover them with the marinara sauce.

4. Lock the Pressure Lid into place, making sure the valve is set to Seal. Select Pressure and adjust the pressure to High and the Cooking Time to 5 minutes. Press Start.

5. After cooking, use a quick pressure release. Carefully unlock and remove the Pressure Lid.

6. Cover the eggplant slices with the mozzarella cheese.

7. Close the Crisping Lid. Select Bake /Roast and adjust the temperature to 375°F and the Cooking Time to 2 minutes. Press Start.

8. When cooking is complete, open the lid and sprinkle the eggplant and cheese with the panko mixture. Close the Crisping Lid again. Select Bake /Roast and adjust the temperature to 375°F and the Cooking Time to 8 minutes. Press Start. When done, the topping should be brown and crisp; if not, broil for 1 to 2 minutes more. Serve immediately.

Nutrition: Calories: 434, Total fat: 20g, Saturated fat: 11g, Cholesterol: 52mg, Sodium: 906mg, Carbohydrates: 47g, Fiber: 8g, Protein: 18g

Mediterranean White Bean Salad

Preparation Time: 10 Minutes

Cooking Time: 30 Minutes

Servings: 4

Ingredients:

- 1 tablespoon plus 1 teaspoon kosher salt (or 2 teaspoons fine salt), divided
- 14 ounces dried cannellini beans
- 4 tablespoons plus 1 teaspoon extra-virgin olive oil, divided
- 1-quart water
- 3 tablespoons freshly squeezed lemon juice
- 1 teaspoon ground cumin
- ¼ teaspoon freshly ground black pepper
- 1 medium red or green bell pepper, chopped (about 1 cup)
- 1 large celery stalk, chopped (about ½ cup)
- 3 or 4 scallions, chopped (about 1 /3 cup)
- 1 large tomato, seeded and chopped (about ½ cup)
- ½ cucumber, peeled, seeded, and chopped (about ¾ cup)
- 1 cup crumbled feta cheese (optional)
- 2 tablespoons minced fresh mint
- ¼ cup minced fresh parsley

Directions:

1. In a large bowl, dissolve 1 tablespoon of kosher salt (or 1½ teaspoons of fine salt) in 1 quart of water. Add the beans and soak at room temperature for 8 to 24 hours.
2. Drain and rinse the beans. Place them in the inner pot. Add 1 teaspoon of olive oil and stir to coat the beans. Add the 1 quart of water and ½ teaspoon of kosher salt (or ¼ teaspoon of fine salt).
3. Lock the Pressure Lid into place, making sure the valve is set to Seal. Select Pressure and adjust the pressure to High and the Cooking Time to 5 minutes. Press Start.
4. While the beans cook and the pressure releases, in a small jar with a tight-fitting lid, combine the lemon juice and 3 tablespoons of olive oil. Add the cumin, the remaining ½ teaspoon of kosher salt (or ¼ teaspoon of fine salt), and the pepper. Cover the jar and shake the dressing until thoroughly combined. (Alternatively, whisk the dressing in a small bowl, but it is easier to make it in a jar.)
5. After cooking, let the pressure release naturally for 10 minutes, then quickly release any remaining pressure. Carefully unlock and remove the Pressure Lid.
6. Drain the beans and pour them into a bowl. Immediately pour the dressing over the beans and toss to coat. Let cool to room temperature, stirring occasionally.
7. Add the bell pepper, celery, scallions, tomato, cucumber, and feta cheese (if using; omit for a dairy-free and vegan dish) to the beans. Toss gently. Right before serving, add the mint and parsley and toss to combine.

Nutrition: Calories: 489, Total fat: 16g, Saturated fat: 2g, Cholesterol: 0mg, Sodium: 622mg, Carbohydrates: 66g, Fiber: 27g, Protein: 25g

Cajun Twice-Baked Potatoes

Preparation Time: 10 Minutes

Cooking Time: 45 Minutes

Servings: 4

Ingredients:

- 4 small russet potatoes, scrubbed clean
- ¼ cup heavy (whipping) cream
- ¼ cup sour cream
- ½ cup chopped roasted red pepper
- 1 teaspoon Cajun Seasoning Mix or a store-bought mix
- 1½ cups shredded white Cheddar cheese
- 4 scallions, white and green parts, chopped, divided
- 1 /3 cup grated Parmesan or similar cheese

Directions:

1. Pour 1 cup of water into the inner pot. Place the Reversible Rack in the pot in the lower position and place the potatoes on top.
2. Lock the Pressure Lid into place, making sure the valve is set to Seal. Select Pressure and adjust the pressure to High and the Cooking Time to 10 minutes. Press Start.
3. After cooking, let the pressure release naturally for 5 minutes, then quickly release any remaining pressure. Carefully unlock and remove the Pressure Lid.
4. Using tongs, transfer the potatoes to a cutting board. When cool enough to handle, slice off a ½-inch strip from the top, the long side of each potato. Scoop the flesh into a large bowl, including the flesh from the tops. Add the heavy cream and sour cream. Using a potato masher, mash until smooth. Stir in the roasted red pepper, seasoning, and Cheddar cheese. Set aside about 2 tablespoons of the green part of the scallions and stir the rest into the potatoes. Spoon the mashed potato mixture into the potato skins, mounding it slightly. Sprinkle the Parmesan evenly over the tops.
5. Empty the water out of the inner pot and return it to the base.
6. Place the Cook & Crisp™ Basket into the pot. Close the Crisping Lid. Select Air Crisp and adjust the temperature to 375°F and the time to 2 minutes to preheat. Press Start.
7. When it is heated, open the lid, and place the potatoes in the basket. Close the Crisping Lid. Select Air Crisp and adjust the temperature to 375°F and the Cooking Time to 15 minutes. Press Start.
8. When done, the potatoes should be lightly browned and crisp on top. Let cool for a few minutes and serve garnished with the reserved scallions.

Nutrition: Calories: 429, Total fat: 25g, Saturated fat: 15g, Cholesterol: 80mg, Sodium: 418mg, Carbohydrates: 35g, Fiber: 3g, Protein: 18g

"Spanish" Rice and Beans

Preparation Time: 5 Minutes

Cooking Time: 30 Minutes

Servings: 4

Ingredients:

- 3 tablespoons olive oil
- 1 small onion, chopped (about 2 /3 cup)
- 2 large garlic cloves, minced
- 1 jalapeño pepper, seeded and chopped (about 2 tablespoons)
- 1 cup long-grain white rice, thoroughly rinse
- 1 /3 cup red salsa
- ¼ cup tomato sauce
- ½ cup Roasted Vegetable Stock, low-sodium vegetable broth, or water
- 1 teaspoon Mexican /Southwestern Seasoning Mix, or store-bought mix
- 1 (16-ounce) can pinto beans, drained and rinsed
- 1 teaspoon kosher salt (or ½ teaspoon fine salt)
- 1 tablespoon chopped fresh cilantro (optional)

Directions:

1. On your Ninja Grill, select Sear /Sauté and adjust to Medium to preheat the inner pot. Press Start. Allow the pot to preheat for 5 minutes. Pour in the olive oil and heat until shimmering. Add the onion, garlic, and jalapeño. Cook for 2 minutes, stirring occasionally, or until fragrant and beginning to soften. Stir in the rice, salsa, tomato sauce, vegetable stock, seasoning, pinto beans, and salt. (If using water, add another ½ teaspoon of kosher salt or ¼ teaspoon of fine salt).

2. Lock the Pressure Lid into place, making sure the valve is set to Seal. Select Pressure and adjust the pressure to High and the Cooking Time to 6 minutes. Press Start.
3. After cooking, let the pressure release naturally for 10 minutes, then quickly release any remaining pressure. Carefully unlock and remove the Pressure Lid. Stir in the cilantro (if using) and serve.

Nutrition: Calories: 384, Total fat: 12g, Saturated fat: 2g, Cholesterol: 0mg, Sodium: 1089mg, Carbohydrates: 60g, Fiber: 7g, Protein: 10g

Best Cream of Broccoli Soup

Preparation Time: 10 Minutes

Cooking Time: 35 Minutes

Servings: 6

Ingredients:

- 1 onion, chopped
- 3 cups of chicken broth
- 3 tablespoons of all-purpose flour
- 5 tablespoons of butter, divided
- 1 stalk celery, to be chopped
- 8 cups of broccoli florets
- Ground black pepper to taste
- 2 cups of milk

Direction:

1. Melt the 2 tablespoons of butter in a medium-size stockpot, and sauté celery and onion until they become tender. Add broth and broccoli, cover, and let it simmer for about 10 minutes.
2. Pour the soup into a blender and make sure the pitcher is not filled more than half full. Hold down the blender lid with a folded kitchen towel and carefully start the blender, use a few quick pulses to get the soup moving, and after that, leave it on the puree.

Then puree in batches until they become smooth and transfer into a clean pot. Alternatively, you can still use a stick blender, but you will have to puree the soup right inside the cooking pot.

3. Melt 3 tablespoons of butter in a small saucepan using medium heat, stir in the all-purpose flour and add milk. Stir until it becomes thick and bubbly and add it to the soup. Season with pepper and serve.

Nutrition: Calories 207,2, Carbohydrates 17 grams 6%, Protein 9.2 grams 18%, Fat 12.4 grams 19%, Cholesterol 31.9 mg 11%, Sodium 528mg 21%.

Spicy Rice with Chickpeas

Preparation Time: 15 Minutes

Cooking Time: 40 Minutes

Servings: 4

Ingredients:

- 1 onion, sliced
- 175g of basmati rice, to be rinsed
- 1 sweet potato, should be peeled and chopped into small chunks
- 25g sultanas
- 3 tablespoons of chopped fresh coriander
- 1 tablespoon of vegetable oil
- 3 tablespoons of medium curry paste
- 500ml of vegetable stock, hot
- 4 medium-size tomatoes, should be chopped
- 400g of can chickpeas, should be drained and rinsed
- 50g of unsalted cashews, should be roughly chopped

Direction:

1. Put the oil in a large pan and heat, then fry the onion over medium heat for 7-8 minutes, stirring until it becomes pale

golden. Add the curry paste and stir-fry for like 1 minute.

2. Stir in the rice and add the sweet potato, stock, sultanas, and tomatoes. Get it to boil and then reduce the heat to a simmer. Cover the pan and leave it on low heat for about 20-25 minutes, frequently stirring until the rice becomes tender and the stock is absorbed. Add more stock if the mixture gets to dry before the rice becomes cooked.

3. Stir in the chickpeas, and gently heat. Stir in the coriander, then season to taste and include enough cashew nuts to serve.

Nutrition: Calories 207.2, Carbohydrates 17 grams 6%, Protein 9.2 grams 18%, Fat 12.4 grams 19%, Cholesterol 31.9 mg 11%, Sodium 528mg 21%.

Summer Veggie Salad

Preparation Time: 20 Minutes

Cooking Time: 1 hour 25 Minutes

Servings: 8

Ingredients:

- 1 (15 ounces) can of black beans, to be rinsed and drained
- 1 bunch of fresh cilantro, should be roughly chopped
- ¼ large red onion should be thinly sliced
- 5 ears of corn, husked
- 2 avocados, California avocados, or NS as to Florida, should be diced
- 1 pint of cherry tomatoes, should be halved
- 1 jalapeno pepper, to be seeded and chopped
- 2 lime (2" Dias) limes, Zested and juiced
- 1.4 cups of olive oil

Direction:

1. Place the corn inside a large pot and cover with water until it boils. Reduce the heat to medium-low and simmer until it becomes tender in about 5 minutes. Drain and cool the corn. Cut kernels from the cob.

2. Mix corn kernels, avocados, black beans, tomatoes, cilantro, jalapeno pepper, and onion altogether in a neat bowl.

3. Whisk lime juice, lime zest, and olive oil together in a bowl. Pour the corn mixture and toss for it to coat. Refrigerate until it becomes chilled in about an hour.

Nutrition: Calories 282.1, Carbohydrates 34.4 grams 11%, Protein 7.7 grams 16%, Fat 15.5 grams 24%, Sodium 228.2mg 9%

High-Protein Vegan Tofu & Mushroom Stir-Fry Recipe

Preparation Time: 15 Minutes

Cooking Time: 55 Minutes

Servings: 4

Ingredients:

- 100g of shiitake mushrooms
- 50g of sugar snap peas
- 30g of edamame beans
- 1 tablespoon of rice vinegar
- 1 clove of garlic
- 100g of beansprouts
- 50g of broccoli
- 1 teaspoon of ginger paste
- 1 teaspoon of soy sauce
- 1 tablespoon of sesame seeds
- 150g of tofu, diced
- ½ teaspoon of sesame oil
- ½ teaspoon of chili flakes
- 100g of mixed vegetables (cabbage, carrots, red onion)

Direction:

1. Mix the soy sauce, ginger paste, garlic, sesame oil, and sesame seeds.
2. Add the diced tofu to the mix and make sure to cover it very well. Wrap with cling film and refrigerate for not less than 30 minutes to marinade.
3. Add the tofu to a pan and cook for about 3-5 minutes.
4. Then add the edamame beans and vegetables and stir fry together for an additional 5 minutes.
5. Serve with sliced red chili and fresh coriander.

Nutrition: Calories: 501, Carbs: 15g, Protein: 38.4g, Fat: 32g

Sauteed Cauliflower Delight

Preparation Time: 15 Minutes

Cooking Time: 30 Minutes

Servings: 4

Ingredients:

- 1 red onion, to be chopped
- 1 cup of cherry tomatoes
- 1 teaspoon of white sugar
- ¼ cup of olive oil
- 1 head of cauliflower, to be cut into florets
- 2 tablespoons of raisins
- 1 clove of garlic, to be minced
- ¼ teaspoon of red pepper flakes
- 1 teaspoon of dried parsley
- 1 tablespoon of fresh lemon juice

Direction:

1. Put the olive oil in a large skillet and heat over medium heat. Cook and stir the onion until it becomes tender in about 5 to 10 minutes. Add cherry tomatoes, cauliflower, raisins, onion, and white sugar, cover the skillet, and cook while frequently stirring until the cauliflower becomes tender in about 4 to 5 minutes.
2. Mix the parsley, garlic, and red pepper flakes inside the cauliflower mixture. Increase the heat to high and sauté until the cauliflower becomes brown in about 1-2 minutes—drizzle lemon juice over the cauliflower.

Nutrition: Calories 196.5, Carbohydrates 17.8 grams 6%, Protein 3.7 grams 8%, Fat 13.9 grams 21%, Sodium 49.2mg 2%

Brown Rice Stir-Fry with Vegetables

Preparation Time: 10 Minutes

Cooking Time: 45 Minutes

Servings: 2 to 4

Ingredients:

- 1 cup (80 g) of chopped cabbage
- ½ cup (100 g) of uncooked brown rice
- ½ chopped red bell pepper
- ½ head of chopped broccoli
- 2 tablespoons of extra virgin olive oil
- ½ cup of chopped zucchini
- 1 handful of fresh parsley, should be finely chopped
- 4 cloves of minced garlic
- 2 tablespoons of tamari or soy sauce
- 1 /8 teaspoon of cayenne powder
- Sesame seeds for garnishing (optional)

Direction:

1. Check the direction on the brown rice and cook as directed
2. Put some water in a frying pan or wok and let it boil. After it boils, add the veggies (note that the water must cover these veggies) and cook for about 1-2 minutes on high heat. Drain the veggies and put them aside.
3. Heat the oil in the wok and add cayenne powder, parsley, and garlic.

Cook with high-heat for 1-minute stirring frequently.

4   Add the rice, vegetables, and tamari—Cook for like 1-2 minutes or more.
5   Add some sesame seeds if you like for garnishing (optional)
6   Store the brown rice stir-fry in a sealed container in the fridge for about 5 days.

Nutrition: 197kcal of Calories, 5.6 grams of protein, 28.1 grams of carbohydrates, 7.9 grams of fat, 1.1 grams of saturated fat, 3.5 gram of sugar, 4.1 grams of fiber, 476.8 milligrams of sodium

Broccoli and Cheese Calzone

Preparation Time: 15 Minutes

Cooking Time: 35 Minutes

Servings: 4

Ingredients:

- 8 ounces of shredded part-skim mozzarella cheese
- Black pepper
- Salt
- 1 (15-ounce) container of part-skim ricotta cheese
- 1 (10-ounce) package broccoli florets, to be thawed and drained
- 2 tablespoons of grated parmesan
- 1 pound of bread or pizza dough, to be thawed

Direction:

1   Get a medium bowl, then combine mozzarella, ricotta, and broccoli. Mix very well. Then season with black pepper and salt
2   Roll dough to a 12-inch circle. Spread the cheese to fill 1 side of the circle to about a 1-inch edge. Lift 1 side of the dough and fold over in other to meet the other side and form a half-moon and pinch the edges together to create a seal.

3   Preheat the oven to about 400°F.
4   Transfer the calzone to a large baking sheet and sprinkle it with cheese. Bake for 15 minutes until it becomes golden brown. Allow it to stand for 15 minutes before you slice.

Nutrition: 207.2 Calories, Carbohydrates 17 grams 6%, Protein 9.2 grams 18%, Fat 12.4 grams 19%, Cholesterol 31.9 mg 11%, Sodium 528mg 21%.

Roasted Spicy Potatoes

Preparation Time: 15 minutes

Cooking Time: 25 minutes

Servings: 4

Ingredients:

- 1 lb. baby potatoes, sliced into wedges
- 2 tablespoons olive oil
- Salt to taste
- 1 tablespoon garlic powder
- 1 tablespoon paprika
- ½ cup mayonnaise
- 2 tablespoons white wine vinegar
- 2 tablespoons tomato paste
- 1 teaspoon chili powder

Directions:

1.   Toss potatoes in oil.
2.   Sprinkle with salt, garlic powder, and paprika.
3.   Add a crisper plate to the air fryer basket.
4.   Add a basket to the Ninja Foodi Grill.
5.   Set it to Air Fry. Set it to 360°F for 30 minutes.
6.   Press Start to preheat.
7.   Put the potatoes on the crisper plate after 3 minutes.
8.   Cook for 25 minutes.
9.   While waiting, mix the remaining ingredients.
10. Toss potatoes in spicy mayo mixture and serve.

Nutrition: Calories: 178, Fat: 10 g, Saturated Fat: 5 g, Carbohydrates: 39 g, Fiber: 6 g, Sodium: 29 mg, Protein: 5 g

Nutrition: Calories: 168, Fat: 12 g, Saturated Fat: 3 g, Carbohydrates: 13 g, Fiber: 1 g, Sodium: 392 mg, Protein: 6 g

Delicious Broccoli and Arugula

Preparation Time: 10 minutes

Cooking Time: 12 minutes

Servings: 4

Ingredients:

- Pepper as needed
- ½ teaspoon salt
- Red pepper flakes
- 2 tablespoons extra virgin olive oil
- 1 tablespoon canola oil
- ½ red onion, sliced
- 1 garlic clove, minced
- 1 teaspoon Dijon mustard
- 1 teaspoon honey
- 1 tablespoon lemon juice
- 2 tablespoons parmesan cheese, grated
- 4 cups arugula, torn
- 2 heads broccoli, trimmed

Directions:

1. Preheat your Ninja Foodi Grill to Max and set the timer to 12 minutes.
2. Take a large-sized bowl and add broccoli, sliced onion, and canola oil, toss the mixture well until coated.
3. Once you hear the beep, it is preheated.
4. Arrange your vegetables over the grill grate, let them grill for 8-12 minutes.
5. Take a medium-sized bowl and whisk in lemon juice, olive oil, mustard, honey, garlic, red pepper flakes, pepper, and salt.
6. Once done, add the prepared veggies and arugula to a bowl.
7. Drizzle the prepared vinaigrette on top, sprinkle a bit of parmesan.
8. Stir and mix.
9. Enjoy!

Grilled Cauliflower Steak

Preparation Time: 30 minutes

Cooking Time: 25 minutes

Servings: 2

Ingredients:

- 2 cauliflower steaks
- ¼ cup vegetable oil, divided
- Salt and pepper to taste
- 1 onion, chopped
- 3 cloves garlic, minced
- ½ cup roasted red bell peppers, chopped
- ¼ cup Kalamata olives, chopped
- 1 tablespoon fresh parsley, chopped
- 1 tablespoon fresh oregano, chopped
- ½ lb. feta cheese, crumbled
- 1 tablespoon lemon juice
- 1 /4 cup walnuts, chopped

Directions:

1. Add grill grate to your Ninja Foodi Grill.
2. Choose the Grill setting.
3. Set it to Max for 17 minutes.
4. Press Start to preheat.
5. Brush both sides of cauliflower steaks with oil.
6. Season with salt and pepper.
7. Grill for 10 minutes per side.
8. Mix the remaining ingredients in a bowl.
9. Spread mixture on top of the steaks and cook for another 2 minutes.

Nutrition: Calories: 240, Fat: 11 g, Saturated Fat: 3 g, Carbohydrates: 33 g, Fiber: 4 g, Sodium: 259 mg, Protein: 6 g

Eggplant Parmesan II

Preparation Time: 25 Minutes

Cooking Time: 1 Hour

Servings: 10

Ingredients:

- ½ cup of grated parmesan cheese. It needs to be divided
- 1 (16 ounces) package of mozzarella cheese. You will need to shred it and divide it.
- 4 cups of Italian-seasoned breadcrumbs
- 3 eggplants, to be peeled and should give about 1.25 pounds of eggplant.
- 2 large eggs, to be beaten
- 6 cups of spaghetti sauce, divided
- ½ teaspoon of dried basil

Direction:

1. Preheat the oven to 350°F (175°C)
2. After you have preheated the oven as required, you will need to open the egg and put the already sliced eggplant and after that, you do the same for the bread crumbs. Then, put it on the baking sheet (single layer). Then, use about 5 minutes for each of the sides to bake inside the oven (remember it must have been preheated).
3. For this step, you will need a 9x13 inch baking dish, inside it, you will put the spaghetti sauce. Then, you will put a single piece of the eggplant slices inside the prepared sauce. Add parmesan cheese and mozzarella. You will need to follow this procedure for all other ingredients but do for the cheeses last. Then sprinkle basil at the top.
4. Is to bake in the preheated oven, this should last for about 35 minutes or when you observe that it has become golden brown.

Nutrition: 487.4 calories, Carbohydrates 62.1 grams 20%, Protein 24.2 grams 48%, Fat 16 grams 25%, Cholesterol 72.8 mg 24%, Sodium 1663.1mg 67%

Broccoli and Torn Arugula

Preparation Time: 10 minutes

Cooking Time: 12 minutes

Servings: 4

Ingredients:

- 4 cups arugula, torn
- 2 heads broccoli, trimmed into florets
- 1 tablespoon lemon juice
- 1 teaspoon honey
- 2 tablespoons parmesan cheese, grated
- ½ red onion, sliced
- 1 tablespoon canola oil
- 1 teaspoon Dijon mustard
- 1 garlic cloves, minced
- 2 tablespoons extra-virgin olive oil
- ¼ teaspoon of sea salt
- Red pepper flakes
- Black pepper, freshly ground

Directions:

1. Insert the grill grate and close the lid
2. Pre-heat Ninja Foodi by pressing the "GRILL" option and setting it to "MAX."
3. Set the timer to 12 minutes
4. Add broccoli, sliced onions, canola oil into a large bowl
5. Toss until coated well
6. Let it pre-heat until you hear a beep
7. Arrange the vegetables over the grill grate and lock lid
8. Cook for 8 to 12 minutes
9. Add lemon juice, mustard, olive oil, honey, garlic, red pepper

flakes, salt, and pepper into a medium bowl
10. Whisk them together
11. Once cooked, combine the roasted vegetables and arugula in a large serving bowl
12. Drizzle with the vinaigrette to taste and sprinkle with parmesan cheese
13. Serve and enjoy!

Nutrition: Calories: 168, Fat: 12 g, Saturated Fat: 3 g, Carbohydrates: 13 g, Fiber: 1 g, Sodium: 392 mg, Protein: 6 g

Toasty Broccoli

Preparation Time: 10 minutes

Cooking Time: 15 minutes

Servings: 3

Ingredients:

- 1 large broccoli head, cut into florets
- 2 tablespoons parmesan, grated
- ½ teaspoon red pepper flakes
- 2 tablespoons extra virgin olive oil
- ¼ cup toasted almonds, sliced
- Lemon wedges
- Pepper and salt to taste

Directions:

1. Add broccoli into a mixing bowl
2. Season with salt and pepper
3. Then add red pepper flakes and toss well
4. Pre-heat Ninja Foodi by pressing the "AIR CRISP" option and setting it to "390 Degrees F."
5. Set the timer to 15 minutes
6. Let it pre-heat until you hear a beep
7. Arrange a reversible trivet in the Grill Pan, arrange broccoli crisps in the trivet
8. Roast it for 15 minutes

9. Add cheese on top and some lemon wedges
10. Serve and enjoy!

Nutrition: Calories: 181, Fat: 11 g, Saturated Fat: 3 g, Carbohydrates: 9 g, Fiber: 4 g, Sodium: 421 mg, Protein: 8 g

Exciting Olive and Spinach

Preparation Time: 10 minutes

Cooking Time: 15 minutes

Servings: 3

Ingredients:

- 2 pounds spinach, chopped and boiled
- 4 tablespoons butter
- 2/3 cup Kalamata olives, halved and pitted
- 1 and ½ cups feta cheese, grated
- 4 teaspoons lemon zest, grated
- Pepper and salt to taste

Directions:

1. Add spinach, butter, salt, pepper into a mixing bowl
2. Mix them well
3. Pre-heat Ninja Foodi by pressing the "AIR CRISP" option and setting it to "340 Degrees F."
4. Set the timer to 15 minutes
5. Let it pre-heat until you hear a beep
6. Arrange a reversible trivet in the Grill Pan
7. Arrange spinach mixture in a basket and place basket in the trivet
8. Roast it for 15 minutes
9. Serve and enjoy!

Nutrition: Calories: 250, Fat: 18 g, Saturated Fat: 3 g, Carbohydrates: 8 g, Fiber: 4 g, Sodium: 339 mg, Protein: 10 g

Italian Rosemary Potatoes

Preparation Time: 10 minutes

Cooking Time: 20 minutes

Servings: 4

Ingredients:

- 2 pounds baby red potatoes, quartered
- ¼ cup onion flakes, dried
- ½ teaspoon parsley, dried
- ¼ teaspoon celery powder
- 2 tablespoons extra virgin olive oil
- ½ teaspoon garlic powder
- ½ teaspoon salt
- ½ teaspoon onion powder
- ¼ teaspoon freshly ground black pepper

Directions:
1. Add all listed ingredients into a large bowl
2. Toss well and coat them well
3. Pre-heat your Ninja Foodi by pressing the "AIR CRISP" option and setting it to 390 Degrees F
4. Set the timer to 20 minutes
5. Allow it to pre-heat until you hear a beep
6. Once preheated, add potatoes to the cooking basket
7. Close the lid and cook for 10 minutes
8. Shake the basket
9. Cook for 10 minutes more
10. Cook for 5 minutes more if needed
11. Serve and enjoy!

Nutrition: Calories: 232, Fat: 7 g, Saturated Fat: 1 g, Carbohydrates: 39 g, Fiber: 6 g, Sodium: 249 mg, Protein: 4 g

Shishito Pepper Charred

Preparation Time: 10 minutes

Cooking Time: 10 minutes

Servings: 4

Ingredients:

- 3 cups Shishito peppers
- 2 tablespoons vegetable oil
- Salt to taste
- Pepper to taste

Directions:

1. Select GRILL mode and set your Ninja Foodi Grill to "MAX."
2. Set timer to 10 minutes
3. Let it pre-heat until you hear a beep
4. Transfer pepper to grill grate and press peppers down and lock lid
5. Cook for 8-10 minutes
6. Once done, serve with some salt and pepper sprinkled on top
7. Serve and enjoy!

Nutrition: Calories: 83, Fat: 7 g, Saturated Fat: 2 g, Carbohydrates: 5 g, Fiber: 1 g, Sodium: 49 mg, Protein: 11 g

Honey-Licious Asparagus

Preparation Time: 10 minutes

Cooking Time: 15 minutes

Servings: 4

Ingredients:

- 2 pounds asparagus, trimmed
- 4 tablespoons tarragon, minced
- ¼ cup honey
- 2 tablespoons olive oil

- 1 teaspoon salt
- ½ teaspoon pepper

Directions:

1. Add asparagus, oil, salt, honey, pepper, tarragon into your bowl
2. Toss them well
3. Pre-heat your Ninja Foodi by pressing the "GRILL" option and setting it to "MED."
4. Set the timer to 8 minutes
5. Let it pre-heat until you hear a beep
6. Arrange asparagus over the grill grate
7. Lock the lid
8. Cook for 4 minutes
9. Then flip asparagus
10. Cook for 4 minutes more
11. Serve and enjoy!

Nutrition: Calories: 240, Fat: 15 g, Saturated Fat: 3 g, Carbohydrates: 31 g, Fiber: 1 g, Sodium: 103 mg, Protein: 7 g

Stuffed Up Cheesy Zucchini

Preparation Time: 10 minutes

Cooking Time: 8 minutes

Servings: 3

Ingredients:

- 1 zucchini
- 1 teaspoon olive oil
- ½ teaspoon tomato paste
- 5 ounces parmesan, shredded
- ½ teaspoon chili flakes
- ¼ teaspoon basil, dried

Directions:

1. Take zucchini and cut into halves, scoop out the flesh from them

2. Spread tomato paste inside the halves
3. Add shredded cheese, sprinkle with chili flakes, dried basil, and olive oil
4. Pre-heat Ninja Foodi by pressing the "AIR CRISP" option and setting it to 375 Degrees F
5. Set the timer to 8 minutes
6. Let it pre-heat until you hear a beep
7. Arrange the prepared zucchini halves in Ninja Foodi Grill Basket
8. Cook for 8 minutes
9. Serve and enjoy!

Nutrition: Calories: 300, Fat: 21 g, Saturated Fat: 1 g, Carbohydrates: 6 g, Fiber: 1 g, Sodium: 459 mg, Protein: 12 g

Blissful Simple Beans

Preparation Time: 5 minutes

Cooking Time: 10 minutes

Servings: 4

Ingredients:

- 1-pound green beans, trimmed
- 1 lemon, juiced
- 2 tablespoons vegetable oil
- Flaky sea salt as needed
- Fresh ground black pepper as needed
- Pinch of red pepper flakes

Directions:

1. Add green beans into a medium-sized bowl
2. Pre-heat your Ninja Foodi by pressing the "GRILL" option and setting it to "MAX."
3. Set the timer to 10 minutes
4. Allow it to pre-heat until you hear a beep
5. Once preheated, transfer green beans to Grill Grate

6. Close the lid
7. Grill for 8-10 minutes
8. Toss them from time to time until all sides are blustered well
9. Squeeze lemon juice over green beans
10. Top with red pepper flakes
11. Season with salt and pepper
12. Serve and enjoy!

Nutrition: Calories: 100, Fat: 7 g, Saturated Fat: 1 g, Carbohydrates: 10 g, Fiber: 4 g, Sodium: 30 mg, Protein: 2 g

Healthy Fruit Salad

Preparation Time: 10 minutes

Cooking Time: 4 minutes

Servings: 4

Ingredients:

- 1 can (9 ounces) pineapple chunks, drained, juice reserved
- 2 peaches, pitted and sliced
- ½ pound strawberries washed, hulled, and halved
- 1 tablespoon freshly squeezed lime juice
- 6 tablespoons honey, divided

Directions:

1. Add strawberries, pineapple, peaches, and 3 tablespoons, honey, into a large bowl
2. Toss it well
3. Pre-heat Ninja Foodi by pressing the "GRILL" option and setting it to "MAX."
4. Set the timer to 15 minutes
5. Let it pre-heat until you hear a beep
6. Transfer fruits to Grill Grate and lock lid
7. Cook for 4 minutes
8. Add remaining 3 tablespoons of honey, lime juice, 1 tablespoon reserved pineapple juice into a small-sized bowl
9. Once cooked, place fruits in a large-sized bowl and toss with honey mixture
10. Serve and enjoy!

Nutrition: Calories: 178, Fat: 1 g, Saturated Fat: 0 g, Carbohydrates: 47 g, Fiber: 3 g, Sodium: 3 mg, Protein: 2 g

Desserts

Blueberry Lemon Muffins

Preparation Time: 5 minutes

Cooking Time: 10 minutes

Serving: 12

Ingredients:

- 1 tsp. vanilla
- Juice and zest of 1 lemon
- 2 eggs
- 1 C. blueberries
- ½ C. cream
- ¼ C. avocado oil
- ½ C. monk fruit
- 2 ½ C. almond flour

Directions:

1. Mix monk fruit and flour.
2. In another bowl, mix vanilla, egg, lemon juice, and cream. Add mixtures together and blend well.
3. Spoon batter into cupcake holders.
4. Air Frying.
5. Place in the air fryer. Bake 10 minutes at 320 degrees, checking at 6 minutes to ensure you do not over bake them.

Nutrition: Calories 317, Fat 11 g, Protein 3 g, Sugar 5 g

Grilled Pound Cake with Berry Compote

Preparation Time: 5 minutes

Cooking Time: 30 minutes

Serving: 4

Ingredients:

FOR THE POUND CAKE

- 1 cup butter, softened
- 1 cup sugar
- 4 eggs
- 1 tsp. vanilla
- pinch of salt
- 2 cups flour

Directions:

1. Mix the compote ingredients in a saucepan. Bring to a boil, stirring well. Remove from the heat and set aside.
2. In a mixing bowl, mix the butter and sugar until fluffy.
3. Add the eggs one at a time, mixing well between each egg.
4. Add the vanilla and salt.
5. Stir in the flour until well combined, but do not over mix.
6. Scoop and level the pound cake batter out onto a sheet pan.
7. Bake until the cake is golden brown.
8. Once the pound cake is cooled, cut into 3-inch squares.
9. Heat the grill to medium and grill the pound cakes lightly. Serve warm with the compote drizzled over the top.

Nutrition: Calories 317, Fat 11 g, Protein 3 g, Sugar 5 g

Sweet Cream Cheese Wontons

Preparation Time: 5 minutes

Cooking Time: 5 minutes

Serving: 16

Ingredients:

- 1 egg mixed with a bit of water
- Wonton wrappers

- ½ C. powdered erythritol
- 8 ounces softened cream cheese
- Olive oil

Directions:

1. Mix sweetener and cream cheese.
2. Layout 4 wontons at a time and cover with a dish towel to prevent drying out.
3. Place ½ of a teaspoon of cream cheese mixture into each wrapper.
4. Dip finger into egg /water mixture and fold diagonally to form a triangle. Seal edges well.
5. Repeat with theremaining ingredients.
6. Insert the Crisper Basket and close the hood. Select AIR CRISP, set the temperature to 400°F, and set the time to 5 minutes. Select START /STOP to begin preheating.
7. Air frying. Place filled wontons into the air fryer and cook 5 minutes at 400 degrees, shaking halfway through cooking.

Nutrition: Calories 303, Fat 3 g, Protein 1 g, Sugar 4 g

Air Fryer Cinnamon Rolls

Preparation Time: 15 minutes

Cooking Time: 5 minutes

Serving: 8

Ingredients:

- 1 ½ tbsp. cinnamon
- ¾ C. brown sugar
- ¼ C. melted coconut oil
- 1-pound frozen bread dough, thawed

Directions:

1. Layout bread dough and roll it out into a rectangle. Brush melted ghee over the dough and leave a 1-inch border along the edges.

2. Mix cinnamon and sweetener and then sprinkle over dough.
3. Roll dough tightly and slice into 8 pieces. Let sit 1-2 hours to rise.
4. To make the glaze, simply mix ingredients till smooth.
5. Air Frying.
6. Once rolls rise, place into the air fryer and cook for 5 minutes at 350 degrees.
7. Serve rolls drizzled in cream cheese glaze. Enjoy

Nutrition: Calories 390, Fat 8 g, Protein 1 g, Sugar 7 g

Smoked Apple Crumble

Preparation Time: 5 minutes

Cooking Time: 45 minutes

Serving: 4

Ingredients:

Filling

- 4–5 large Honeycrisp apples, peeled and sliced
- juice from ½ lemon
- 2 Tbsp. flour
- 1/3 cup sugar
- 1 Tbsp. ground cinnamon
- 1 tsp. ground nutmeg

Directions:

1. Insert the Grill Grate and close the hood. Select GRILL, set temperature to HIGH, and set time to 40 minutes. Select START /STOP to begin preheating.
2. Place apples in a large mixing bowl and toss with lemon juice. Then add in flour, sugar, cinnamon, and nutmeg, and mix thoroughly.
3. Pour apples into a greased cast-iron pan. Set mixture aside.
4. Using the now-empty mixing bowl, combine brown sugar, flour, oatmeal, caramel chips, pecans, cinnamon, baking powder, and salt for the topping.
5. Using a pastry blender or large fork, cut the cold butter into the topping mix.
6. Cover apples with topping mixture.
7. Add one or two pecan wood chunks to the hot coals. Place apple crumble over the Roasting Rack.
8. Close the hood and bake until apples start to bubble, and topping begins to brown (about 45 minutes.
9. Remove from grill and serve warm with French vanilla ice cream.

Nutrition: Calories 317, Fat 11 g, Protein 3 g, Sugar 5 g

Bread Pudding with Cranberry

Preparation Time: 5 minutes

Cooking Time: 35 minutes

Serving: 4

Ingredients:

- 1-1 /2 cups milk
- 2-1 /2 eggs
- 1 /2 cup cranberries1 teaspoon butter
- 1 /4 cup and 2 tablespoons white sugar
- 1 /4 cup golden raisins
- 1 /8 teaspoon ground cinnamon
- 3 /4 cup heavy whipping cream
- 3 /4 teaspoon lemon zest
- 3 /4 teaspoon kosher salt
- 3 /4 French baguettes, cut into 2-inch slices
- 3 /8 vanilla bean, split and seeds scraped away

Directions:

1. Lightly grease the baking pan of the air fryer with cooking spray. Spread baguette slices, cranberries, and raisins.
2. In a blender, blend well vanilla bean, cinnamon, salt, lemon zest, eggs,

sugar, and cream. Pour over baguette slices. Let it soak for an hour.
3. Cover pan with foil.
4. For 35 minutes, cook at 330°F.
5. Let it rest for 10 minutes. Serve and enjoy.

Nutrition: Calories 590, Fat 25 g, Protein 17 g, Sugar 9 g

Black and White Brownies

Preparation Time: 10 minutes

Cooking Time: 20 minutes

Serving: 8

Ingredients:

- 1 egg
- ¼ cup brown sugar
- 2 tablespoons white sugar
- 2 tablespoons safflower oil
- 1 teaspoon vanilla
- ¼ cup of cocoa powder
- 1/3 cup all-purpose flour
- ¼ cup white chocolate chips
- Nonstick baking spray with flour

Directions:

1. In a medium bowl, beat the egg with the brown sugar and white sugar. Beat in the oil and vanilla.
2. Add the cocoa powder and flour and stir just until combined. Fold in the white chocolate chips.
3. Spray a 6-by-6-by-2-inch baking pan with nonstick spray. Spoon the brownie batter into the pan.
4. Bake for 20 minutes or until the brownies are set when lightly touched with a finger. Let cool for 30 minutes before slicing to serve.

Nutrition: Calories 317, Fat 11 g, Protein 3 g, Sugar 5 g

French toast Bites

Preparation Time: 5 minutes

Cooking Time: 15 minutes

Serving: 8

Ingredients:

- Almond milk
- Cinnamon
- Sweetener
- 3 eggs
- 4 pieces of wheat bread

Directions:

1. Insert the Crisper Basket and close the hood. Select AIR CRISP, set the temperature to 360°F, and set the time to 15 minutes. Select START /STOP to begin preheating.
2. Whisk eggs and thin out with almond milk.
3. Mix 1 /3 cup of sweetener with lots of cinnamon.
4. Tear bread in half, ball up pieces, and press together to form a ball.
5. Soak bread balls in egg and then roll into cinnamon sugar, making sure to thoroughly coat.
6. Air frying. Place coated bread balls into the air fryer and bake for 15 minutes.

Nutrition: Calories 300, Fat 10 g, Protein 2 g, Sugar 4 g

Baked Apple

Preparation Time: 5 minutes

Cooking Time: 20 minutes

Serving: 4

Ingredients:

- ¼ C. water

- ¼ tsp. nutmeg
- ¼ tsp. cinnamon
- 1 ½ tsp. melted ghee
- 2 tbsp. raisins
- 2 tbsp. chopped walnuts
- 1 medium apple

Directions:

1. Insert the Crisper Basket and close the hood. Select AIR CRISP, set the temperature to 350°F, and set the time to 20 minutes. Select START /STOP to begin preheating.
2. Slice the apple in half and discard some of the flesh from the center.
3. Place into the frying pan.
4. Mix the remaining ingredients except for water. Spoon mixture to the middle of apple halves.
5. Pour water overfilled apples.
6. Air frying. Place pan with apple halves into the air fryer, bake 20 minutes.

Nutrition: Calories 205, Fat 11 g, Protein 2 g, Sugar 5 g

Coffee and Blueberry Cake

Preparation Time: 5 minutes

Cooking Time: 35 minutes

Serving: 6

Ingredients:

- 1 cup white sugar
- 1 egg
- 1 /2 cup butter, softened
- 1 /2 cup fresh or frozen blueberries
- 1 /2 cup sour cream
- 1 /2 teaspoon baking powder
- 1 /2 teaspoon ground cinnamon
- 1 /2 teaspoon vanilla extract
- 1 /4 cup brown sugar
- 1 /4 cup chopped pecans
- 1 /8 teaspoon salt

- 1-1 /2 teaspoons confectioners' sugar for dusting
- 3 /4 cup and 1 tablespoon all-purpose flour

Directions:

1. In a small bowl, whisk well pecans, cinnamon, and brown sugar.
2. In a blender, blend well all wet ingredients. Add dry Ingredients except for confectioner's sugar and blueberries. Blend well until smooth and creamy.
3. Lightly grease the baking pan of the air fryer with cooking spray.
4. Pour half of the batter into the pan. Sprinkle half of the pecan mixture on top. Pour the remaining batter. And then topped with the remaining pecan mixture.
5. Cover pan with foil.
6. For 35 minutes, cook at 330°F.
7. Serve and enjoy with a dusting of confectioner's sugar.

Nutrition: Calories 480, Fat 26 g, Protein 5 g, Sugar 8 g

Cinnamon Sugar Roasted Chickpeas

Preparation Time: 5 minutes

Cooking Time: 10 minutes

Serving: 2

Ingredients:

- 1 tbsp. sweetener
- 1 tbsp. cinnamon
- 1 C. chickpeas

Directions:

1. Insert the Crisper Basket and close the hood. Select AIR CRISP, set the temperature to 390°F, and set the time to 10 minutes. Select START /STOP to begin preheating.

2. Rinse and drain chickpeas.
3. Mix all ingredients and add to the air fryer.
4. Air frying. Cook 10 minutes.

Nutrition: Calories 115, Fat 20 g, Protein 18 g, Sugar 7 g

Cherry-Choco Bars

Preparation Time: 5 minutes

Cooking Time: 15 minutes

Serving: 8

Ingredients:

- ¼ teaspoon salt
- ½ cup almonds, sliced
- ½ cup chia seeds
- ½ cup dark chocolate, chopped
- ½ cup dried cherries, chopped
- ½ cup prunes, pureed
- ½ cup quinoa, cooked
- ¾ cup almond butter
- 1 /3 cup honey
- 2 cups old-fashioned oats
- 2 tablespoons coconut oil

Directions:

1. Insert the Crisper Basket and close the hood. Select AIR CRISP, set the temperature to 375°F, and set the time to 15 minutes. Select START /STOP to begin preheating.
2. In a mixing bowl, combine the oats, quinoa, chia seeds, almond, cherries, and chocolate.
3. In a saucepan, heat the almond butter, honey, and coconut oil.
4. Pour the butter mixture over the dry mixture. Add salt and prunes.
5. Mix until well combined.
6. Pour over a baking dish that can fit inside the air fryer.
7. Air frying. Cook for 15 minutes.
8. Let it cool for an hour before slicing into bars.

Nutrition: Calories 330, Fat 15 g, Protein 7 g, Sugar 8 g

Cinnamon Fried Bananas

Preparation Time: 5 minutes

Cooking Time: 10 minutes

Serving: 2-3

Ingredients:

- 1 C. panko breadcrumbs
- 3 tbsp. cinnamon
- ½ C. almond flour
- 3 egg whites
- 8 ripe bananas
- 3 tbsp. vegan coconut oil

Directions:

1. Heat coconut oil and add breadcrumbs. Mix around 2-3 minutes until golden. Pour into a bowl.
2. Peel and cut bananas in half. Roll the half of each banana into flour, eggs, and crumb mixture.
3. Air Frying. Place into the air fryer. Cook 10 minutes at 280 degrees.
4. A great addition to a healthy banana split!

Nutrition: Calories 215, Fat 11 g, Protein 5 g, Sugar 5 g

Chocolate Granola

Preparation Time: 5 minutes

Cooking Time: 1 hr. 50 mins

Servings: 8

Ingredients:

- 2 cups flaked almonds
- cup slivered almonds

- 1 cup unsweetened shredded coconut
- 1/4 cup coconut oil, melted
- 1/3 cup Surkin melis
- 1/4 cup unsweetened cocoa powder

- 3 egg whites

Directions:

1. Preheat your Ninja to 250F. Line a cookie sheet with wax paper.
2. In a large bowl, add both the almonds, coconut, coconut oil, and mix well. Sift the Surkin melis and cocoa powder into the almond mixture. Mix well.
3. In a separate bowl, whisk the eggs for 2-3 minutes until foamy, then pour into the nut mixture. Mix well.
4. Spread over the prepared cookie sheet. Bake for 1 hour, checking and stirring every 10 mins. The mixture should look dry and the almonds, lightly browned.
5. Remove from the oven and leave to cool for 45 mins. Once cooled, store in an airtight jar.

Nutrition: Calories 380, Total fats 35 g, Fiber 8 g, Carbs 12 g, Protein 11 g

Molten Lava Cake

Preparation Time: 5 minutes

Cooking Time: 3 hr. 10 mins

Servings: 6

Ingredients:

- 1.5 cup Swerve sweetener
- 1/2 cup gluten-free flour
- 5 tbsp unsweetened cocoa powder & 2 cups hot water
- 1/2 tsp salt & liquid vanilla stevia
- 1 tsp baking powder & vanilla
- 1/2 cup butter melted cold
- 3 whole eggs & 3 egg yolks

- 4-ounce chocolate chips

Directions:

1. In a large bowl, whisk together 1 1/4 cup Swerve, flour, 3 tbsp cocoa powder, salt, and baking powder. In another small bowl, stir the cooled melted butter, eggs, yolk, vanilla extract, and liquid stevia.
2. Add the wet ingredients into dry ingredients until combined and pour this into a greased Ninja Foodi pot. Top with chocolate chips.
3. Whisk the remaining 2 tbsp cocoa powder and the remaining Swerve sweetener with hot water.
4. Pour over the top of the chocolate chips. Cover cook on low for 3 hours.
5. Allow cooling before serving.

Nutrition: Calories 157, Total fats 13 g, Fiber 5.7 g, Carbs 10.5 g, Protein 3.9 g

Keto Lemon Cake

Preparation Time: 5 minutes

Cooking Time: 3 hr. 10 mins

Servings: 12

Ingredients:

- 1.5 cup almond flour
- 1/2 cup coconut flour
- 3 tbsp all-purpose flour
- 2 tsp baking powder & 2 eggs
- 1/2 tsp xanthan gum (optional)
- 1/2 cup melted butter & whipping cream, each
- Juice & zest from 2 lemons

Directions:

1. Combine almond flour, coconut flour, sweetener, baking powder, and xanthan gum in a bowl.
2. Whisk together butter, whipping cream, zest, and eggs in a bowl.

3. Add dry mix to wet and combine until well blended. Line Ninja Foodi with aluminum foil.
4. Combine all topping items in a bowl and pour over cake batter in Ninja. Cover cook on high setting for about 2-3 hrs. Serve warm with fruit and whipped cream, if desired.

Nutrition: Calories 350, Total fats 33 g, Fiber 4 g, Carbs 11 g, Protein 7.6 g

Carrot Cake

Cooking Time: 4 hr.

Servings: 6

Preparation Time: 5 minutes

Ingredients:

- 1 tsp ground cinnamon
- 3 /4 cup swerve sweetener
- 1 /2 cup shredded coconut, almond flour & chopped pecans
- 1 /4 cup unflavored protein powder
- 2 tsp baking powder
- 1 /4 tsp ground cloves & salt
- 2 cups grated carrots
- 4 large eggs, 1 /2 tsp vanilla
- 1 /4 cup kelapo coconut oil
- 3 tbsp almond milk

Directions:

1. Line your Ninja with parchment paper, grease parchment paper.
2. In a bowl, whisk together the sweetener, almond flour, shredded coconut, protein powder, chopped nuts, baking powder, cloves, cinnamon, and salt.
3. Add the shredded carrots, eggs, coconut oil, almond milk, and vanilla extract until well incorporated. Spread the batter in prepared Ninja and cook on low for 3 to 3 ½ hours.

4. Frost with desired frosting, cooled.

Nutrition: Calories 348, Total fats 30.6 g, Fiber 2 g, Carbs 9.5 g, Protein 9.6 g

Lemon Berry Cake

Preparation Time: 5 minutes

Cooking Time: 3 hr. 15 min

Servings: 4

Ingredients:

- 6 eggs
- 1/2 cup coconut flour
- 1/3 cup lemon juice& 2 tsp zest
- 1 tsp lemon liquid stevia
- 1/2 cup Swerve sweetener
- 2 cups heavy cream & 1 /2 tsp salt
- 1/2 cup fresh blueberries

Directions:

1. Place the egg whites into a stand mixer and whip until stiff peaks form. Set aside.
2. In another bowl, whisk the yolks and remaining ingredients together except blueberries.
3. Fold egg whites a little at a time into the batter until just combined.
4. Grease your Ninja pot and pour the mixture. Sprinkle the blueberries over the batter.
5. Cover the lid, vent, and cook on low for 3 hours or until a toothpick comes out clean.
6. Allow cooling with the cover off for 1 hour then place in the refrigerator to chill for 2 hours.
7. Serve cold with whipped cream if desired.

Nutrition: Calories 191, Total fats 17 g, Fiber 4 g, Carbs 4 g, Protein 4 g

Pumpkin Custard

Cooking Time: 2 hr. 40 mins

Servings: 2

Preparation Time: 5 minutes

Ingredients:

- 4 large eggs
- 1/2 cup granulated stevia
- cup pumpkin puree
- 1 tsp vanilla extract
- 1/2 cup almond flour
- 1 tsp pumpkin pie spice
- 1/8 tsp sea salt
- 4 tbsp butter

- Grease Ninja Foodi with butter

Directions:

1. Break eggs into a medium mixing bowl. Blend until smooth, and while mixing gradually, add sweetener. Add pumpkin puree and vanilla extract to the egg mixture and blend it.
2. Blend in almond flour, salt, and pumpkin pie spice. Continue to blend in, adding butter. While all ingredients are mixed, transfer to the slow cooker.
3. Place a paper towel between the pot and lid. Cover set to vent and cook for 2 hours and 30 mins.

4. Serve warm with stevia-sweetened whipped cream.

Nutrition: Calories 217, Total fats 5 g, Fiber 0.6 g, Carbs 3 g, Protein 38 g

Bundt Cake

Preparation Time: 5 minutes

Cooking Time: 2 hr. 30 mins

Servings: 7-8

Ingredients:

- 3/4 cup all-purpose flour
- 2/3 cup granulated sugar
- tsp pumpkin pie spice
- 1/2 tsp baking powder, vanilla & soda, each
- 1 large egg
- 1/3 cup yogurt & butter, each
- tsp confectioner's sugar

Directions:

1. Place a coil of the aluminum sheet inside the bottom of your Ninja. Place a greased pan inside it.
2. In a bowl, whisk together the flour, sugar, pumpkin pie spice, baking powder, baking soda, and salt.
3. Add the egg, yogurt, butter, and vanilla to the flour mixture. Use an electric mixer, beat for 1-2 minutes. Scrape the sides. Beat on high speed for 2 mins.
4. Spread batter evenly into pan. Cover, vent, and cook on high for 2-3 hours.
5. Carefully remove, transfer the cake onto a rack to cool.

6. Serve with confectioner's sugar.

Nutrition: Calories 233, Total fats 10 g, Fiber 12 g, Carbs 29 g, Protein 3 g

Cherry Cola Cake

Preparation Time: 5 minutes

Cooking Time: 3 hr. 40 mins

Servings: 12

Ingredients:

- box chocolate cake mix
- 21 ounces canned cake pie filling
- 1.5 cups cola

- 8 ounces cream cheese icing from a 16 ounces store-bought container

Directions:

1. Turn your Ninja Foodi on and place cherry pie filling, spreading evenly.

2. Spread the cake mix as a layer, spread evenly, and as smooth as possible on the cherry pie filling.

3. Slowly add the cola over the dry cake mix, ½ cup at a time. Make sure all the dry cake mix is covered with the cola.

4. Cover the lid, vent, and cook on HIGH for 3.5 to 4 hours.

5. Turn off the Ninja and allow it to sit uncovered for ½ hr.

6. Serve cake on plates and drizzle with cream cheese icing.

7. Serve with whipped cream or vanilla ice cream as desired.

Nutrition: Calories 415, Total fats 15 g, Fiber 3 g, Carbs 69 g, Protein 4 g

Pumpkin Dump Cake

Preparation Time: 5 minutes

Cooking Time: 2 hr. 15 mins

Servings: 10

Ingredients:

- 15 ounces canned pumpkin puree
- 12 ounces canned evaporated milk
- 4 large eggs
- ½ cups granulated sugar
- tsp pumpkin pie spice
- 1/2 tsp Kosher salt
- 18.25 ounces yellow cake mix
- 1/2 cup butter melted

- 1 cup chopped pecans, optional

Directions:

1. In a bowl, mix pumpkin, evaporated milk, eggs, sugar, pumpkin pie spice, and salt.

2. Add to the bottom of the greased Ninja Foodi pot and spread evenly.

3. Evenly sprinkle dry yellow cake and mix to the top of the pumpkin mixture.

4. Add melted butter evenly over the top of the dry cake mix.

5. Sprinkle top with chopped pecans if using.

6. Cover, vent, and cook on HIGH for 2 hours.

Nutrition: Calories 676, Total fats 33 g, Fiber 1 g, Carbs 88 g, Protein 9 g

Pineapple Dump Cake

Preparation Time: 5 minutes

Cooking Time: 3 hr. 5 mins

Servings: 12

Ingredients:

- 14 ounces undrained canned crushed pineapple
- tbsp granulated sugar
- 1 box yellow cake mix
- 1 cup of butter melted

Directions:

1. Add pineapple to the bottom of the greased Ninja pot.
2. Sprinkle the sugar on the top.
3. Then sprinkle dry cake mix on top of the cake mix.
4. Pour the melted butter slowly over the top.
5. Place a thin, clean kitchen towel between the lid and the slow cooker.
6. Cover the lid and set the valve to the vent position.

7. Cook on HIGH for 3 hours.

Nutrition: Calories 328, Total fats 17 g, Fiber 1 g, Carbs 42 g, Protein 1 g

Peach Dump Cake

Preparation Time: 5 minutes

Cooking Time: 2 hr. 15 mins

Servings: 6

Ingredients:

- 14.5 ounces canned peach
- box yellow cake mix
- 1 cup of butter melted

Directions:

1. Turn on your Ninja Foodi and grease the bottom.
2. Add canned peach with the juice.
3. Sprinkle the dry cake mixes on the top of the peach as evenly as possible.
4. Cover the lid, set to Vent.
5. Cook on HIGH for 2 hours.
6. Frost with favorite frosting.

7. Enjoy!

Nutrition: Calories 619, Total fats 35 g, Fiber 0 g, Carbs 74 g, Protein 3 g

Chocolate Pumpkin Bars

Preparation time: 15 minutes

Cooking time: 3 hours

Serving: 16

Ingredients:

For crust:

- ¾ cup unsweetened coconut, shredded
- ¼ cup cacao powder
- ½ cup raw unsalted sunflower seeds
- ¼ teaspoon salt
- ¼ cup erythritol
- 4 tablespoons butter, softened

For filling:

- 1 (29-ounce) can sugar-free pumpkin puree
- 1 cup heavy cream
- 6 organic eggs
- ½ teaspoon salt
- 1 tablespoon organic vanilla extract
- 1 tablespoon pumpkin pie spice
- 1 teaspoon cinnamon liquid stevia
- 1 teaspoon stevia extract

Direction:

1. Line the pot of ninja food with a greased parchment paper
2. For the crust: in a food processor, add all the ingredients and pulse until fine crumbs like mixture are formed.
3. In the pot of prepared ninja food, place the crust the mixture and press to smooth the top surface.
4. For the filling: in the bowl of a stand mixer, add all ingredients and pulse until well combined.
5. Place the filling over crust evenly.
6. Close the ninja food with a crisping lid and select "slow cooker".
7. Set on "low" for 3 hours.
8. Press "start /stop" to begin cooking.
9. With the help of parchment paper, carefully lift the bars and transfer them onto a wire rack to cool completely.
10. Cut into desired sized bras and serve.

Nutrition: Calories: 121, fats: 9.7g, carbs: 6.3g, Fiber: 2.4g, sugar: 2.2g, proteins: 3.5g

Easy Blueberry Cobbler

Preparation Time: 10 Minutes

Cooking Time: 1 Hour 5 Minutes

Servings: 8

141

Ingredients:

- 1 cup of self-rising flour
- 1 cup of milk
- ½ cup of butter
- 1 cup of white sugar
- 4 cups of fresh blueberries

Direction:

1. Preheat your oven to 350OF (175OC) and put butter to use in an 8-inch square baking dish
2. Then, melt the butter in the preheating oven for like 5 minutes and then remove it from the oven.
3. Mix sugar, flour, and milk in a bowl until they all combine. Then pour the batter over the melted butter and scatter the blueberries over the batter.
4. Bake in the already preheated oven until you insert a toothpick at the center, and it comes out clean in approximately 1 hour.

Nutrition: 310.4 Calories, Carbohydrates 48.5 grams 16%, Protein 3.2 grams 6%, Fat 12.5 grams 19%, Cholesterol 32.9 mg 11%, Sodium 293.4 mg 12%.

Cauliflower Steaks - Roasted

Preparation Time: 10 Minutes

Cooking Time: 30 Minutes

Servings: 4

Ingredients:

- 1 pinch of red pepper flakes
- 1 tbsp. of lemon juice (fresh)
- ¼ cup of olive oil
- 2 cloves of garlic, minced
- 1 pinch of salt and ground black pepper
- 1 cauliflower (large head), sliced vertically into four.

Direction:

1. Preheat the oven to 4000F (2000C). Get parchment paper to line your baking sheet.
2. Put cauliflower steaks on the already prepared sheet.
3. Whisk lemon juice, olive oil, red pepper flakes, garlic, black pepper, and salt inside a small bowl. Then, apply about the half quantity of the olive oil you've already mixed on the cauliflower steaks.
4. Then, in the already preheated oven, you will need to put the cauliflower steaks and roast them for about 15 minutes. Each steak should be turned to the other side and you will then apply the leftover olive oil on it as you did earlier. You will need to roast for about 15-20 minutes when the steaks would become tender with golden color.

Nutrition: 175.8 Calories, Carbohydrates 12.1 grams 4%, Protein 4.3 grams 9%, Fat 13.8 grams 21%, Sodium 63.6 mg 3%.

Grilled Pineapple Butterscotch Sundaes

Preparation Time: 10 Minutes

Cooking Time: 25 Minutes

Servings: 12

Ingredients:

- 2 tablespoons of white sugar
- 2 each of fresh pineapples, to be peeled, cored, and cut into 6 spears
- 1 cup of packed brown sugar
- 6 tablespoons of butter
- ¼ teaspoon of ground nutmeg
- ½ cup of butter
- ½ cup of heavy whipping cream
- 1 pinch of salt
- 1 teaspoon vanilla extract
- 3 cups of vanilla ice cream

Direction:

1. Preheat the grill with medium heat and lightly oil the grate
2. Heat 6 tablespoons of butter, nutmeg, and white sugar in a saucepan on medium heat and stir until the sugar dissolves in about 5 minutes. Then brush the pineapple spears with butter mixture.
3. Arrange pineapple on the already preheated grill and cover, grill until it becomes lightly brown, turning frequently; this should last between 7 to 10 minutes. Then transfer the pineapple to a platter.
4. Get another saucepan and melt the remaining ½ cup of butter using medium heat. Stir in heavy cream and brown sugar, then bring to a boil, stirring as frequently as possible. Remove from the heat and add salt and vanilla extract. Serve the pineapple topped with ice cream and cream sauce.

Nutrition: 388.2 Calories, Carbohydrates 51.9 grams 17%, Protein 2.7 grams 6%, Fat 21 grams 32%, Cholesterol 63.7 mg 21%, Sodium 131.2 mg 5%.

Glazed Carrots

Preparation Time: 10 Minutes

Cooking Time: 15 Minutes

Servings: 8

Ingredients:

- ¼ cup of butter
- ¼ teaspoon of salt
- 2 pounds of carrots, should be peeled and cut into steaks
- ¼ cup of packed brown sugar
- 1 /8 teaspoon of ground white pepper

Direction:

1. Place the carrots into a large saucepan, pour water to reach 1-inch depth, and bring to a boil. Reduce the heat to low, cover, and simmer the carrots until they become tender in about 8-10 minutes. Drain and transfer to a neat bowl.
2. Melt butter in the same saucepan, stir salt, brown sugar, and white pepper into the butter until the salt and sugar have dissolved. Transfer the carrots into brown sugar sauce; cook and keep stirring until the carrots are glazed with the sauce in about 5 minutes.

Nutrition: 123.6 Calories, Carbohydrates 17.6 grams 6%, Protein 1.1 grams 2%, Fat 6 grams 9%, Cholesterol 15.3 mg 5%, Sodium 193.8 mg 8%.

Peanut Butter Banana Melty

Preparation Time: 10 Minutes

Cooking Time: 15 Minutes

Servings: 4

Ingredients:

- ½ cup of peanut butter
- large bananas
- ½ cup of chocolate chips

Direction:

1. Without peeling the bananas, slice each of them vertically. Smear the inside of each of them with peanut butter and sprinkle with chocolate chips. Place the 2 halves back together and wrap each banana individually in aluminum foil.
2. Now cook in the hot coal of a campfire until the banana becomes hot, and the chocolate has melted in about 10-15 minutes (this depends on the level of heat from the coals).

Nutrition: 411.3 Calories, Carbohydrates 50.6 grams 16%, Protein 10.5 grams 21%, Fat 23 grams 35%, Sodium 151.7 mg 6%.

Blueberry Mint Smoothie

Preparation Time: 10 Minutes

Cooking Time: 40 Minutes

Servings: 2

Ingredients:

- 1 cup of water
- 1 avocado, to be peeled and pitted
- 2 teaspoons of lemon juice
- 2 cups of frozen blueberries
- 1 cup of fresh mint leaves
- ½ cup of orange juice

Direction:

1. Blend blueberries, mint leaves, water, avocado, lemon juice, and orange juice in a blender until they become smooth.

Nutrition: 273.2 Calories, Carbohydrates 35 grams 11%, Protein 3.5 grams 7%, Fat 15.9 grams 25%, Sodium 13.1 mg 1%

Classic Dinner Rolls

Preparation Time: 40 Minutes

Cooking Time: 20 Minutes

Servings: 12

Ingredients:

- 1 envelope Fleischmann's® RapidRise Yeast
- ½ teaspoon of salt
- ¼ cup of water
- 2 cups of all-purpose flour or more if necessary
- 2 tablespoons of sugar

- ½ cup of milk
- 2 tablespoons of butter or margarine

Direction:

1. Combine ¾ cup of flour, sugar, undissolved yeast, and salt in a large bowl. Heat butter, water, and milk until they become very warm (1200F-1300F). Then add to the flour mixture. Beat for 2 minutes with a medium speed of electric mixer, scraping the bowl frequently. Add ¼ cup of flour and beat for 2 minutes at high speed. Stir in the remaining flour to make a soft dough. Knead on a lightly floured surface until it becomes smooth and elastic in about 8-10 minutes. Cover and let it rest for about 10 minutes.
2. Divide the dough into 12 equal pieces and shape them into balls. Then put in a greased 8-inch round pan. Cover and let it rise in a warm daft-free place until it becomes doubled in about 30 minutes.
3. Bake in the already preheated 3750F oven for 20 minutes or until it gets done. Remove from the pan and brush with extra melted butter if you like. Serve warm.

Nutrition: 107.9 Calories, Carbohydrates 18.5 grams 6%, Protein 2.8 grams 6%, Fat 2.3 grams 4%, Cholesterol 5.9 mg 2%, Sodium 115.3 mg 5%.

Chantal's New York Cheesecake

Preparation Time: 30 Minutes

Cooking Time: 1 Hour

Servings: 12

Ingredients:

- 2 tablespoons of butter, to be melted
- 1 ½ cups of white sugar
- 4 large eggs

- 15 large rectangular piece or either 2 squares or 4 small rectangular pieces of graham crackers, to be crushed
- 4 (8 ounces) packages of cream cheese
- ¾ cup of milk
- 1 cup of sour cream
- ¼ cup of all-purpose flour
- 4 large eggs
- 1 tablespoon of vanilla extract

Direction:

1. Preheat the oven to 3500F (1750C). Then grease a 9-inch springform pan.
2. Get a medium bowl and mix melted butter with graham cracker crumbs. Then, press on the bottom of the springform pan.
3. Get a large bowl and mix sugar with cream cheese until they become smooth. Blend in milk, and after that, mix the eggs one after the other and let it incorporate. Then mix in vanilla, sour cream, and flour until they become smooth. Then pour filling into the prepared crust.
4. Bake in the already preheated oven for like 1 hour. Turn off the oven and leave the cake to cool in it while the oven door is closed for about 5-6 hours; this is necessary to prevent cracking. Then chill in the refrigerator until you are ready to serve.

Nutrition: 533.4 Calories, Carbohydrates 44.2 grams 14%, Protein 10.3 grams 21%, Fat 35.7 grams 55%, Cholesterol 158.9 mg 53%, Sodium 380.4 mg 15%.

Conclusion

Thanks for making it to the end of this book. Ninja grill cooking is a fun way to eat great food. It's also a great way to get healthier meals, cheaper food, and to get your family involved in the cooking process. Ninja cooker cooking is a great way to simplify your life and to create the freedom and flexibility you need to live the life you want. Remember, the key to becoming a ninja grill cook is to have fun and to stay positive. Once you get started, you'll be amazed at all you can learn about cooking with your ninja grill. You can learn to cook anything on your ninja and even create your amazing recipes.

So, get started and you'll be amazed at all the fun and good food you can create!

CPSIA information can be obtained
at www.ICGtesting.com
Printed in the USA
LVHW112324161121
703564LV00002B/16